UNEARTHED

UNEARTHED

THE LANDSCAPES OF HARGREAVES ASSOCIATES

KAREN M'CLOSKEY

PENN

UNIVERSITY OF PENNSYLVANIA PRESS
Philadelphia

PENN STUDIES IN LANDSCAPE ARCHITECTURE

John Dixon Hunt, Series Editor

This series is dedicated to the study and promotion of a wide variety of approaches to landscape architecture, with special emphasis on connections between theory and practice. It includes monographs on key topics in history and theory, descriptions of projects by both established and rising designers, translations of major foreign-language texts, anthologies of theoretical and historical writings on classic issues, and critical writing by members of the profession of landscape architecture.

The series was the recipient of the Award of Honor in Communications from the American Society of Landscape Architects, 2006.

This book is supported by grants from the Graham Foundation for Advanced Studies in the Fine Arts.

The University of Pennsylvania Press acknowledges the generous funding provided by a David R. Coffin Publication Grant from the Foundation for Landscape Studies, and PennDesign at the University of Pennsylvania.

Published by
UNIVERSITY OF PENNSYLVANIA PRESS
Philadelphia, Pennsylvania 19104-4112
www.upenn.edu/pennpress

Unless otherwise credited, all images courtesy of Hargreaves Associates.

Printed in Canada on acid-free paper
10 9 8 7 6 5 4 3 2 1

Library of Congress Cataloging-in-Publication Data
M'Closkey, Karen.
  Unearthed : the landscapes of Hargreaves Associates / Karen M'Closkey.
— 1st ed.
    p. cm. — (Penn studies in landscape architecture)
  Includes bibliographical references and index.
  ISBN 978-0-8122-4480-9 (hardcover : alk. paper)
  1. Hargreaves Associates—History. 2. Urban landscape architecture—
United States—20th century. 3. Urban landscape architecture—United
States—21st century. 4. Public spaces—United States. I. Title. II. Series:
Penn studies in landscape architecture.
  SB469.9.M35 2013
  712′.5—dc23
                        2012046478

BOOK DESIGN BY JUDITH STAGNITTO ABBATE / ABBATE DESIGN

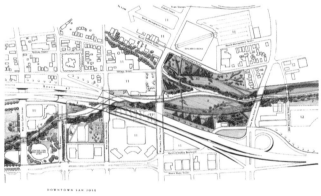

DOWNTOWN SAN JOSE

CONTENTS

FIGURE 2. Molded landforms with redwood trees and misters recall fog emerging from a valley. Prospect Green, Sacramento, California (1990–93).

is considered both material and conceptual or abstract.[19]

In order to clarify this point, discussion of two radically dissimilar practitioners representing radically different interpretations is useful to underscore the efficacy of a "geologic" approach to design: landscape architect Ian McHarg (1920–2001) and architect Peter Eisenman (b. 1932). McHarg and Eisenman, through their writing, design practices, and spirited personae, as well as their canonization by critics and theorists, emblematize a defining moment in their respective disciplines. Despite the limiting, and some would say incapacitating, effects of their design methods, their work continues to provide a baseline for subsequent reformulations of their respective disciplines.[20] Both

used working methods that utilize mapping to mine the substrate for clues. These clues are physical accretions that are brought to the "surface" (represented in their drawings) to materially and culturally ground their work. And though they were certainly not the first to use such methods, they popularized them by making their process legible and, therefore, usable and teachable, which is why each became so influential in his respective field.

When McHarg published his seminal book *Design with Nature* (1969), Eisenman had just finished the first of his series of "cardboard houses" (House I, 1968). Although they were ideologically at opposite ends of the spectrum, both claimed to remove the subjectivities of the designer via their methodology, which relates their work directly to the language of emergence and process used today (in which natural processes, or computer processes, "complete" the work). Furthermore, their opposing definitions of what constitutes "site" illustrate the impossibility of maintaining the claim that a design method can be authorless or value-free. A site's value—what gets privileged and what gets suppressed—is itself a product of the author's agenda and cannot sit outside it, even though the resultant work will be open to multiple interpretations, experiences, and transformations.

GEOMORPHIC MAPPINGS

MCHARG WORKED ON regional planning scales and was deeply committed to environmental health. He also recognized that any landscape is a value-laden territory, which is why he thought an objective method itself was value-free enough to "prove" how development should occur. For McHarg, understanding the existing natural and cultural patterns was essential to producing work considered in the best interest of the largest number of people. He believed the "given form" of the site provided the constraints for the work and that, subsequent to analysis of its natural and cultural patterns, there was an optimal answer to any problem: "There will be a form of fitting which is most fitting."[21] In order to derive the areas most fit for a particular type of development, he used a mapping method comprising a series of transparent overlays. This now well-known method, a precursor to digital geographic information systems, used each layer to represent a different *value*, indicating a limitation imposed on

the site beginning with, for example, underlying bedrock, soil characteristics, hydrology, and places of cultural significance. He mapped each value independently as a tone or color. When the layers were superimposed, the gradient on the composite map "revealed" the area most suited for a particular type of development. In other words, the area with little or no tone had the fewest restrictions on it.[22] McHarg saw these maps as an accurate depiction of the present condition of the site. He believed that a precise definition of context was possible and considered his methodology reproducible by anyone using the same procedure.

GEOMETRIC MAPPINGS

To privilege "the site" as the context is to repress other possible contexts, is to become fixated on the presences of "the site," is to believe that "the site" exists as a permanent, knowable whole.[23]

—PETER EISENMAN

In contrast to the *given form* of the site, Eisenman refers to the *imminent* in every site. He is resolutely against the kind of positivism that characterized McHarg's work. Thus, while McHarg looked for the most suitable fit, Eisenman is interested in misfits. Whether working typologically by dismantling platonic cubes (House Series, 1967–80) as a means to challenge such oversimplified notions as "form follows function," or working contextually by overlaying multiple actual and fictional maps (Cities of Artificial Excavation, 1978–88), Eisenman wishes

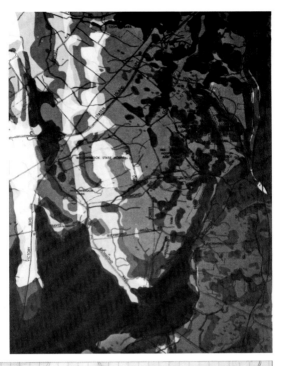

FIGURE 3. McHarg's mapping of physiographic obstructions in order to determine road alignment. Reprinted from McHarg's *Design with Nature* (New York: John Wiley & Sons, 1992). Reprinted with permission of John Wiley & Sons.

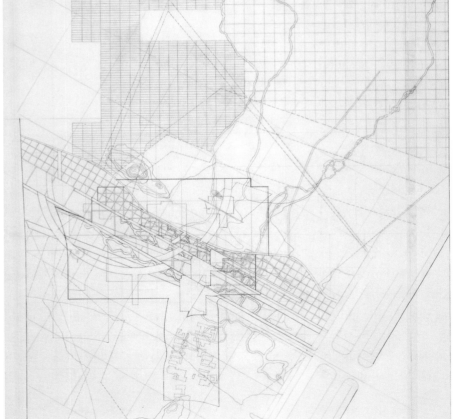

FIGURE 4. A site plan showing various layers superimposed. Image by the Office of Eisenman/ Robertson Architects for Long Beach: University Art Museum of the California State University at Long Beach, 1986. From *Cities of Artificial Excavation: The Work of Peter Eisenman, 1976–1988* (Montreal: Canadian Centre for Architecture and Rizzoli International Publication, 1994). Reprinted with permission of the Canadian Centre for Architecture. Peter Eisenman Fonds, Collection Centre Canadien d'Architecture/ Canadian Centre for Architecture, Montreal.

to destabilize the notion of a valued origin. He has described three fallacious "isms": modernism's nostalgia for the future, postmodernism's nostalgia for the past, and contextualism's nostalgia for the present.[24] In the Cities work, Eisenman traced multiple urban grids that existed at various points in history, unbuilt designs by other architects slated for that particular site, and mappings of invisible characteristics such as noise patterns. He then arbitrarily scaled these geometric abstractions to various sizes and superimposed them in order to create the grounds for his designs. Because these new grounds cannot be traced back to any particular origin, they give no more or less credence to any one time; thus, artificial excavations focus on the elusiveness of the "real" site.

While McHarg used mapping as a *means to an end*, a strategy of avoidance in order to determine where *not* to build, Eisenman's mappings focus on the design process as *endless means*, a strategy of "voidance," where, at least theoretically speaking, there is no identifiable beginning or end to the work.[25] Though both extrapolate from the past, McHarg's work operates primarily through tracing and cataloguing, a procedure based on what he believed to be the predictability and repeatability of the "real." The importance of his work is the implication of every site in relation to its larger physiographic region. Eisenman, on the other hand, eschews any belief in mapping as a manifestation of any fact or truth. The artificial excavations are not seen as descriptions of that which exists, but rather are seen as a series of fragments that do not add up to a more basic or underlying condition. In other words, any combination of map layers is an equally "truthful" account of the context. The usefulness of his practice is that it focuses on the techniques and conventions by which architecture gets made, foregrounding the fact that the "theoretical assumptions of functionalism are in fact cultural rather than universal."[26] Even though they are ideologically opposed (McHarg would be characterized as a positivist, and Eisenman a poststructuralist), both discount subjective experience. McHarg did so in favor of quantifiable criteria about which there is presumed agreement, whereas Eisenman claims to ignore sensual or programmatic opportunities, believing both to be rooted in a humanism that he rejects. So in the end, the design proposals that result from their respective methodologies are described primarily as a snapshot of process.

SITE

> The means are important, but only as to the end they lead to. I have not abandoned process, but rather learned where it belongs through the act of building.[27]
>
> —GEORGE HARGREAVES

Although Hargreaves helped usher in the process-driven approach, equating open-endedness with the unfinished work, he later criticized this approach, as is evident in the above quotation. In other words, Hargreaves does not utilize an unyielding design methodology (where the process is valued over the result) but shares in the ambitions of a "geological" approach that integrates diverse physical and temporal layers. Others have noted Hargreaves's affiliation with Halprin because of

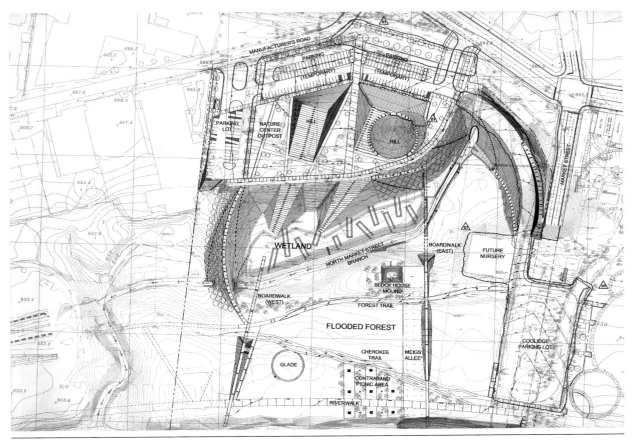

FIGURE 5. A grading plan for Renaissance Park, Chattanooga. Hargreaves Associates' design can be seen with respect to the underlying survey conditions.

Halprin's references to geomorphology. In terms of design method, however, Hargreaves Associates' use of drawing layers gives rise to organization in a way more closely aligned with Eisenman's Cities work than with Halprin's notational drawings. The former are plan-based drawings that overlay multiple layers taken from past points in time; whereas the latter represents temporal processes with a series of marks that capture fleeting or anticipated movement (as in a dance performance).[28] And though Hargreaves was not directly influenced by the pro-

cesses engaged in by either McHarg or Eisenman, the combination of the two distinct ways of using information—material constraints and formal innovation—characterizes Hargreaves Associates' work. This combination of approaches results in a fundamentally different type of practice than either method employed on its own.[29]

In his first published writing, "Post-Modernism Looks beyond Itself" (1983), Hargreaves argues that postmodernism should turn its attention to the physical external reality represented in the map rather than the internalized autonomous space of the grid.[30] As the comparison of McHarg and Eisenman clearly illustrates, maps do not represent reality, they represent a particular reading of it; likewise, Hargreaves's evocation of the map is meant to reference more than the underlying material conditions of a site. He notes the importance of mapping in the form of data collection in McHarg's work, but argues that this resulted in "imitative naturalism" when applied to individual sites.[31] Later, and more in the spirit of Eisenman, Hargreaves describes the firm's approach as a multiscalar "abstract archeology."[32] In other words, the information unearthed from site research is used to give form to the already "given form" of the site, such as when a former artifact or material condition inspires a new organization. This approach accepts that certain material aspects inherent in the site must be considered relative to fitness (such as appropriateness to subsurface conditions, such as soil or saturation levels that will support certain types of vegetation but not others) but that the misfits—formal innovations that cannot be tied to existing conditions—open opportunities for producing new grounds and, subsequently, new experiences and patterns of use. Hargreaves Associates' work thus engages a site's material and cultural histories without using them to reproduce an existing order.

As I emphasize in the next chapter, this approach is utilized as a means to recover "place" in the spaces that economic processes have literally and figuratively leveled. This is not to be misconstrued as an essentialist "genius loci," but rather to foreground that landscapes are temporally and materially multilayered, having gone through continu-

al transformation, especially, and radically, during industrialization. Thus reading a site is not a distillation of its "essence" but rather a projection of possibilities. Transforming the types of sites that landscape architects face today means engaging in an immense amount of research and strategic planning due to a myriad of factors: extant infrastructure and buildings; phasing requirements due to incremental funding; local, state, and federal laws pertaining to contaminated sites; and the multiple and conflicting interests that arise when adapting a site for public use. These physical, financial, and regulatory constraints provide limitations on, and opportunities for, how and where to act. Accordingly, mapping multiple layers of information remains a necessary process for sites of this complexity. However, this alone will not create a unique or memorable environment. Many of these sites are devoid of the natural features that gave character, spatial interest, and temporal depth to the parks of the nineteenth century. Because of this condition, the grounds for the project must be largely manufactured, and this requires great facility in working the ground.

FORM

HARGREAVES PLACES considerable emphasis on complexly graded topography, where the conspicuous articulation of the ground organizes movement, orientation, and different zones of use. In many of the firm's projects, the earthwork is predominant. Some landforms are characterized by geometrically nameable forms, such as cones or spirals, some are inspired by natural formations, some from past uses on the site, and others have no referent at all; however, in all cases, such forms are clearly human-made. Landscape historian John Dixon Hunt notes that in our current intellectual milieu, which includes an increased awareness and concern for humans' impact on the environment, we witness a return to the prominence of geomorphological representations in landscape architecture. Hunt warns that we should be careful not to mask the "fictions" of our creations because "it is precisely in that modern, ecological instance that we confront once again what may be called the Brownian fallacy. By insisting on naturalistic design, landscape architects run the risk of effacing themselves and their art."[33] Likewise, even though Hargreaves Associates' work utilizes earth, water, and vegetation as the primary structuring elements (in conjunction with all the unseen physical supports that make these landscapes possible, such as retaining and utilities), the firm's approach to molding the ground reflects an effort to resist naturalization.

This tendency is supported by a working method: the firm relies heavily on physical models made from clay. Working with such material enables the designer to bypass the limits of drawing and develop a facility for working the ground in complex ways. Clay models are not images in the way that drawings or diagrams are. The clay is not notational or pictorial; rather, it is a transformable, malleable, and homogenous substance. Rather than representing movement through notational drawings, or representing temporality through indexing past traces, the clay enables the designer to focus on the form of the ground and the importance of sectional change

for guiding movement—of people and water—and creating spaces. Though Hargreaves Associates designs are now also developed through computer modeling, the firm continues to use clay, especially early in a project's formation. When Hargreaves was chair of the landscape architecture department at Harvard, the clay landform workshop was a mandatory part of the curriculum, and involved molding the ground into precise, measured forms. Students were asked to utilize multiple forms in configurations where they would abut, intersect, and overlap so as to compel the student to understand the complex intersections of different slopes and shapes. As noted by Kirt Rieder, an associate at Hargreaves Associates who ran the workshop for eight years, "the emphasis on distinct forms and pronounced intersections between these surfaces runs counter to the prevailing attitude in landscape architecture to 'soften' or blend grading into the existing conditions to make new interventions appear seamless or solely as background scenery."[34] This working method resists an imitative naturalism by creating unique and prominent topography. Though this aspect of the work has been described as "mimetic" because some of the earthwork resembles forms produced by natural processes, or "decorative" because it represents such processes without always engaging them directly, neither adequately explains the effect of the topography in terms of the relationships set up by the ground's organization, a topic further explored in the third chapter ("Effects").[35]

FIGURES 6-8. Various study models made of malleable materials. Candlestick Point Park was designed collaboratively with the architect and artist using a sandbox model (opposite, top). Parque do Tejo e Trancao in Lisbon, Portugal (opposite, bottom), and Saint-Michel Environmental Complex in Montreal, Quebec (above), are clay models.

MATERIAL: REGISTRATION AND RESISTANCE

GIVEN THE CHARACTERIZATION of Hargreaves Associates' early work, and Hargreaves's own statements about process, what role does this notion play in the firm's work in terms of its detailing and construction? The ability to see processes registered on site has as much to do with fixed form as it does with the changing aspects of a landscape; therefore, it is as much concerned with *ends* as with *means*. "Resistance" involves the material, construction, and maintenance procedures that uphold the landscape's structure and appearance over time, whereas "registration" refers to the ability to see change within or against this structure. Both are necessary and they function together. The recognizable figures and compositions in Hargreaves Associates' work are designed and built to resist the erosive power of water or large crowds, their edges constructed with gabions (rock-filled cages) or concrete or reinforced with geotextiles (subsurface fabrics) or ground-cover planting. In terms of natural processes, Hargreaves Associates' approach favors addressing a cyclical time frame of daily tides, seasonal color, or seasonal flooding, for example, rather than a linear time frame of succession and growth. These are obviously not exclusive of each other (cyclical events gradually transform the landscape); however, they offer distinct approaches when used as the basis for design. For example, Hargreaves believes that in garnering support from clients and public, complete construction of distinct portions of a project is more effective than treating an entire site evenly or proposing successional landscapes that are presumed to grow in. He acknowledges that some areas have to be "let go," but only so that the limited financial resources can be focused on other aspects of a project.[36] Thus, in most of the work, phasing and zoning assure that a uniformly distributed character does not evolve across the site. There are areas where material processes are highlighted, for example, the break in the river wall in Louisville Waterfront Park, where the registration of water flow is visible because of the debris that collects in the inlets and the gradient of vegetation that results. But it also remains visible because one side of the cut is reinforced to maintain a distinct edge. Even in areas that are not subject to flooding or large volumes of water, many of the earthworks in Hargreaves Associates' projects are reinforced with geotextiles in order to maintain their distinct forms and resist gradual processes of erosion.

There are early projects that invoke succession, and it is worth looking at these to see how they have fared in comparison to the later projects that utilize more distinct zones and with higher maintenance budgets. The power of projects such as Candlestick Point Park and Byxbee Park, both of which involved collaborations with artists, derives from the subtle differences between the constructed site and the surrounding landscape of sky and sea, arising from the use of simple incisions that register water levels, or markers that orient the view outward. These parks were restrained by design, but they were also constrained by budget and maintenance, installed for between one and two dollars per square foot. Their locations are peripheral to their city centers (San Francisco and Palo Alto, Calif., respectively) in areas with previous industrial or landfill uses. The site conditions are similar to those that have formed the basis of more recent and well-publicized projects. The questions frequently asked in recent publications are: How much design is enough? How can a master plan be avoided? How do maintenance concerns bear on design? Do investing less up front and being less specific about design result in greater flexibility for future use? It has been over twenty years since Candlestick Point and Byxbee Parks were constructed; therefore, Hargreaves Associates' work offers interesting case studies to consider these questions.

Candlestick Point Park is 18 acres of land within the 170-acre Candlestick Point State Recreational Area. Hargreaves Associates' original intent was a

FIGURE 9. Candlestick Point Park, showing one of the tidal inlets in the foreground soon after construction. The stepped gabion walls that retain the central mown grass figure can be seen.

FIGURE 10. Candlestick Point Park showing the same inlet in 2004. Photograph by the author.

FIGURE 11. Aerial view of Candlestick Point Park from 2008 showing the vegetation encroaching on the central figure and the tidal inlets filled with sediment and vegetation. Image courtesy of the U.S. Geological Survey.

heightened contrast between the irrigated grasses that form the central lawn and the adjacent meadow left to its own cycles of growth and a lack of irrigation.[37] The distinction between the two zones is less visible now, as nature has been allowed to take its course because of infrequent maintenance. Though still occasionally mown, the formerly pristine central lawn is dotted with shrubs. The maintenance crews who mow this area maneuver around the shrubs, allowing additional species to colonize the untouched pockets, further eroding the distinc-

tion between the lawn and the adjacent ground. Activities originally envisioned for the site have not taken place because the associated building was never funded. The site is sparsely populated, and there are graffiti on the concrete outcroppings by the water's edge. Part of its appeal, at least to a one-time visitor, is its rough appearance and deserted feeling, which makes the presence of the bay that much more commanding. Located a half-mile walk from the nearest neighborhood, it is surrounded by a sea of asphalt that is the 49ers' stadium parking lot.

There is no question that Candlestick Point Park is a critical project for the discipline of landscape architecture, as it eschewed a verdant nature to which the field had become accustomed; however, the lack of funding and minimal program development are not within the control of the designer, so why would these aspects be celebrated as a desirable or inevitable state of landscape design today, as is evident in the winning scheme for Downsview Park Toronto by OMA/Bruce Mau?[38] Though the proposal appeared to be a brilliant polemic, it is an emergent scheme because design specifics were suppressed in favor of managerial organizations that would eventually evolve the project. Not surprisingly, the plan that inevitably resulted from this process is a very banal and uninspired landscape.

Designed just after Candlestick Point Park, and located thirty miles south and east of it, is Byxbee Park. Also planted with native grasses, the covered sanitary landfill contrasts seasonally to the marsh below, "swapping" colors during the seasons: when one is green in winter and spring, the other is golden, with the inverse true in the summer. The original species selection was a choice made by Hargreaves Associates based on its survivability without irrigation and the desired visual effects; however, the grasses must be maintained through the removal of colonizing species that would otherwise likely overtake them, even though the colonizing plants are obviously well adapted to the site's harsh conditions.[39] In fact, there has been little success with removal of these plants.[40] Nor did the processes that were presumably set in motion transpire; for example, where concrete curbs were placed parallel to the ground's contours to presumably collect water on their upward side and prompt growth of more wa-ter-loving vegetation. So while landscape is often called the art of time, it is also aptly described as the art of maintenance.

The widespread emphasis on process that was prevalent after Hargreaves Associates finished these first projects acknowledges that sites are inevitably open to change, but using this knowledge requires understanding the existing conditions that are likely to enable particular changes to occur, changes that also imply particular forms of maintenance. The next chapter (regarding Crissy Field) further addresses this topic, as does Chapter 2, "Techniques." The topic brings to the fore the often conflicting notions of sustainability: the acknowledgment that landscapes are inherently open to change, coupled with the desire to "sustain" a particular type of landscape in response to specific social and programmatic demands.

CONCLUSION

RECENT DISCUSSIONS in landscape architecture have tended to emphasize two dominant, yet contradictory, aspects of landscape: its changing and unpredictable nature and its known and "performative" functions ("performative" is a term often used to describe what a project "does"—the effects that it sets in motion—rather than what it "is"—its physical form, materials, appearance). The fact that these are at odds remains unacknowledged, for example, when successional models of growth are used to show how biodiversity builds over time. Even though disturbances, such as floods and fires, are recognized, projects are still presumed to move to-

INTRODUCTION

ward a more complex state ecologically. Likewise, the social equivalent to emergence presumes that if we design less, it automatically leaves more room for users to change or appropriate a space. How does Hargreaves Associates' work fit these two characterizations?

The dynamism of natural processes' effects on design intentions is most visible in a project like Candlestick Point Park described above; however, the lack of initial funding and minimal design did not allow it to "evolve" into a more complex landscape. Now, with plans to demolish the 49ers stadium and the area slated for large development, a larger and more generic park, designed by AECOM, will replace Hargreaves Associates' design. Other projects will not share its fate anytime soon, as the nature of the projects Hargreaves Associates has undertaken has changed.[41] Rather than having construction budgets of one dollar per square foot, projects such as Louisville Waterfront Park or Chattanooga Waterfront Park are investing twenty to twenty-five times that amount per acre of park development, with construction phased anywhere from five to twenty years, and per-acre maintenance budgets exceeding that of New York's Central Park.[42] Hargreaves Associates is involved not only with the planning of the landscape but also with the plans that financially underwrite the landscape development, including helping clients create the 501c organizations that will help fund and maintain their projects. These projects require immense investments from both public and private sources, and the "open space" commonly associated with the public realm is reciprocally tied to the funding mechanism for private development. In several of

FIGURE 14. The twelve-acre Discovery Green in Houston, Texas, is an example of a densely programmed site, funded largely with private money for its land, construction, and maintenance. Previously a sparsely populated site comprising mainly parking and lawn, it has become a destination that has enlivened the downtown area and attracted new development.

Hargreaves Associates' projects, the private investment catalyzed by the park development was from two to four and a half times greater than the funds for the initial public infrastructure.[43] So there is no question that these projects "perform" economically by enticing development and raising property values.

In addition to the event-based programs, such as concerts, that these landscapes support, many comprise complex infrastructures. Their projects are designed such that flood control and stormwater treatment systems are interwoven with cultural and recreational events. The environmental criteria are measured, whereas the firm's multifunctional design tactic enables other program elements—terraces,

FIGURES 12 AND 13. Byxbee Park in Palo Alto, California, showing the seasonal color "swap" of the marsh and park grasses.

FIGURE 15. Louisville Waterfront Park during a large event, April 21, 2007. Image courtesy of Michael Schnuerle.

sible. Many projects are funded not only through a city's open-space allocations, or the eventual return from private development and tourist taxes, but through state and federal funding.[44]

Finally, the public process by which land is transformed into public space is often where the debate over site use and management happens because many people need to buy into these projects, emotionally, intellectually, and financially. One tactic is to leave the design so open that it will be created by committee or by managers, such as at Downsview Park. Fortunately, Hargreaves does not confuse lack of specificity with flexibility. To claim that formal or material indeterminacy is any more liberating or communal than what modernists claimed about space, or postmodernists about surface, is to fall prey to the same fallacy—that there is a direct cause and effect between a designer's intent and a project's reception, eventual use, and control.[45] Funding, maintenance, ownership, and restriction of uses have little to do with a particular form or aesthetic. However, designers do propose surfaces, materials, and forms that can enable or preclude particular uses.

For example, a large swath of lawn, irrespective of whether it is embedded in Olmsted's nineteenth-century picturesque Central Park or Hargreaves Associates' late twentieth-century Louisville Waterfront Park, provides a place for large gatherings, protests, temporary memorials, games, and so on; therefore, its use is open, but its form is precise, its material is uniform and soft, and its size is pertinent to supporting a range of activities (Central Park's Great Lawn is fifteen acres; the lawn at Louisville Waterfront Park is twelve acres). The fact that protestors were not allowed to use Central Park's Great

large event spaces, theatrical displays of water, or small seating areas—to exist in tandem with the more utilitarian ones. In this sense, combining the measurable function of landscape, such as water control, with recreation is a strategic way to make public space because more total funds are allocated to the project and more area is made publicly acces-

Lawn for demonstrations in 2004 lest it ruin the grass is a problem of ownership and permitting, rather than of form or material.[46] Had the entire site been designed as a rocky ramble of intimate, winding paths, which would have precluded large gatherings, it would have been a problem of form and material. In other words, design determines "openness" in very specific ways. The language of emergence as applied to landscape architecture risks valuing change for change's sake. Perhaps this sentiment should not be surprising, as it is an outgrowth of concerns and critiques that began four decades ago when the slippery relationships among authorship, representation, and reception became widely problematized. However, the notion that less design, or more open-endedness, affords greater flexibility should be seen as a critique of the role of designers and planners (and the social assumptions underlying their designs) rather than an empower-ment of those who would presumably take over such undesigned spaces.

The point of this introduction to Hargreaves Associates' work is not to simply suggest replacing *ecology* with *geology* as a metaphor for design method; however, if we are to adopt a "complexity theory" for landscapes, it should not be a complexity theory of self-organizing systems (such as nature), or one that positions design as the inevitable outcome of forces beyond the designer's control, which is already part and parcel of any built project. Hargreaves Associates' work makes a compelling case that facility in dealing with given conditions does not equate to a conservative replication of those conditions, nor do given conditions alone suffice to define the work. They do, however, provide the foundation, as well as inspiration, for the expressive, programmatic, and aesthetic agendas layered onto a site's given form and material.

Chapter 1

GEOGRAPHIES

Geographical "place" is today treated as an instantiation of process
rather than an ontological given. This way of thinking about spatial scale
immediately reintroduces matters of time and history into geography.

— DENIS COSGROVE

LOCAL SPACES ARE TIED TO REGIONAL AND GLOBAL PROCESSES. SPATIAL SHIFTS, INCLUDING THE RECENT AVAILABILITY OF LARGE SWATHS OF DERELICT LAND IN UR- BAN AREAS, ARE THE RESULT OF INTERSECTING ECONOMIC AND POLITICAL FORCES

that influence a region's transformation over time. The parks being made on such sites today are implicated in these larger processes in two ways: first, the space for their existence is enabled by the movement of manufacturing to other regions and countries, as well as military base closures, resulting in the so-called postindustrial landscape; second, the funding for their existence is enabled by revitalization efforts that are used to entice capital into city centers—as real estate development and tourist dollars—since parks play a major role in "urban renewal."[1] In other words, the transformation of derelict land into parks is as much a product of shifting capital as was the prior abandonment of the same land.[2]

Though today's park landscapes serve similar functions to their nineteenth-century counterparts in that they are infrastructural, combining hydrology, transportation, and recreation, they are radically different in how their social and ecological functions are defined. In an era marked by increased awareness of the global environmental impact of human actions, attention to environmental justice, and mandated public processes for design implementation, the task of developing appropriate proposals for such sites is not easy, particularly because the "public" is not the unified subject or body that it was presumed (or desired) to be in the nineteenth century. Parks are no longer seen as a means to "solve" social ills or educate the "lower" classes by means of bourgeois aesthetic standards; yet parks remain culturally, socially, and ecologically significant. How can the work of landscape architects successfully represent a diverse collective of people who privilege different aspects of a site's past events or future uses without catering to the demands of a single group or neglecting those whose interests may not be part of the client's sanctioned agenda? How do landscape architects design for socially diverse groups in a way that can support differences without compartmentalizing public space into exclusive zones that cater to only one group or use the hegemonic approaches that characterized much modern planning? How is "place" recovered or defined in the spaces that have been stripped of their natural features and severed from their surroundings?

George Hargreaves's response to these challenges is through explicating what he refers to as the "rich history of the ground."[3] The projects highlighted in this chapter show how this notion informs the firm's work in various ways that allow it to engage the history of sites without sentimentalizing the past on the one hand, or simply ignoring it on the other. This chapter analyzes how Hargreaves Associates responds to the physical and cultural layers that constitute these sites, which includes identifying former uses or events that are deemed significant, and how these are recognized in the designs. Thus, the theme of "Geographies" focuses on how the firm's design approach reintroduces "matters of time and history" into public landscapes.

REPRESENTING THE COLLECTIVE

Planners, architects, urban designers,—"urbanists" in short—all face one common problem: how to plan the construction of the next layers in the urban palimpsest in ways that match future wants and needs without doing too much violence to all that has gone before. What has gone before is important precisely because it is the locus of collective memory, of political identity, and of powerful symbolic meanings at the same time as it constitutes a bundle of resources constituting possibilities as well as barriers in the built environment for creative social change.[4]

—DAVID HARVEY

THE PIONEERING MODERNISTS COULD NOT foresee that the shifting location and quantity of manufacturing labor, along with legislation supporting centrifugal development, would lead to an exodus of industry and population from cities, leaving gaps and detritus that would form the sites for future landscape architects. The result of post–World War II urban disinvestment is a landscape that has been described variously as *holey*, *dross*, *void*, *terrain vague*, and so on, and, as architect Albert Pope notes, is "characterized as where people are not, where the urban collective is profoundly marked or inscribed by its absence."[5] It is well known that these gaps resulted from federal policies. Until the 1970s, numerous federal housing acts supported new construction, rather than rehabilitation, resulting in the destruction of neighborhoods that were deemed blighted.[6] Moreover, the 1956 Federal Highway Act gave local planners the jurisdiction to cut highway routes through their cities as well as 90 percent of the funds needed for their construction, eroding the building fabric, displacing people, and isolating neighborhoods. We are familiar with the results of these discriminatory procedures because the pattern was repeated throughout American urban environments. Not surprisingly, these late-modern-era clearing operations prompted much skepticism about the efficacy of planning, contributing to current theorizing about the death of the master plan. Many are doubtful of the potential for master plans to do more than kowtow to formalized and traditional notions of creating community: "It is better to suffer the void of abstraction than gratuitous representation, better to be lost than to languish in the 'objective world' of closed urban development."[7]

Attempts to redress the abuses of modernism's clearing operations—when it was presumed that the correct spatial form (ordered and clean) equated to a correct social form (ordered and clean)—have been varied. On the one hand is the return to some presumably shared past through the use of historical symbols that cater to a nostalgic idea of "community." This is seen in much New Urbanist work and is what the above quote by Pope, as well as landscape urbanism in the United States, is positioned against.[8] As cultural geographer David Harvey notes, community is a "mythical social entity," which can be as much a part of the problem as a panacea (as in gated "communities," or any exclusionary group).[9] The other extreme, as suggested by Pope and others, is to adopt an approach of "letting it be," where the past returns as an imagined form of unmediated nature. Some have suggested that these vacated spaces should remain as they are because their value lies in their lack of definition. Abandoned leftover spaces, where natural processes overtake cultural artifacts, are seen to offer conceptual alternatives to the colonizing forces of the marketplace. Their lack of productivity or purpose results in a "crisis of classification" and in this crisis apparently lies freedom: freedom from the capitalist forces that produced these sites in the first place.[10] As noted in the introduction, Hargreaves Associates' Candlestick Point Park shares some of these qualities of entropy and decay that some find so appealing.

The contrast between these two extremes (exclusionary planning versus lack of planning) reveals two distinct approaches to what Harvey identifies as a perpetual pendulum swing between *utopianisms of spatial form* and *utopianisms of process*. Though his example of a utopianism of process is the laissez-faire of the free market (the belief that if the market were truly free from regulation all would be right and well), the "let it be" of the terrain vague and some recent projects within landscape design are equally utopias of process, where design specificity is suppressed in favor of letting projects "naturally" evolve (as seen in OMA/Mau's winning scheme for Downsview Park in Toronto). An alternative approach is to assume that public space remains vital and to ask not whether we should reconfigure these spaces, but how. If the move toward isolated pockets of urban disinvestment was underwritten by economic and environmental policies, the same should be true of efforts to reinhabit these urban voids. And if such development is to reflect more than gratuitous representation, it should begin with acknowledging the changed nature of design and planning today, which is a more publicly engaged process than in the era of tabula rasa modernism. As a result, the questions of representation and community are not entirely abstract ones.[11] In other words, the process by which public space gets made today is radically different than in the eras that preceded it. While others are right to challenge the kind of development that often happens on newly available sites, development that privatizes and limits access, leaving them isolated from the public sphere (or doing very little and presuming they will evolve into something complex) is not an alternative to addressing the open-space needs of residents. As Harvey notes, "to materialize a space is to engage with closure (however temporary) which is an authoritarian act. . . . The problem of closure (and the authority it presupposes) cannot endlessly be evaded. To do so is to embrace an agonistic romanticism of perpetually unfulfilled longing and desire."[12]

What other design approaches can speak to a landscape's regional or cultural identity without capitulating to the consumable images found in our increasingly commodified environments or, on the contrary, leaving a site as is rather than engaging in active construction, thereby sentimentalizing the deterioration that results from neglect? The following examples show various ways that Hargreaves Associates has created public landscapes that stitch together diverse aspects of their milieus while creating new identities for these places. The firm's approach to unearthing the rich history of the ground avoids both the homogenizing grounds of modern-era development and the romanticizing of ruins left in its wake.

ACKNOWLEDGMENT

THE PRINCIPLE of acknowledgment is central to Hargreaves Associates' design approach.[13] Acknowledgment is not a tactic concerned with known symbols or typologies that relies on public engagement through a presumably shared system of signification. Although an early statement by George Hargreaves—"Pluralism is appropriate. The expression of symbolism, mysticism, and humanism will become a preoccupation"—might suggest such an approach, the way his work engages these concerns is more complex than resorting to eclecticism by pillaging and collaging symbols in an attempt to construct a seemingly congruent lineage for a place (for example themed environments such as nautical motifs along a waterfront).[14] This question of how to "ground" the site is of particular concern given the conditions where landscape architects work today. Hargreaves notes that the parks of past centuries had inherent complexity given their extant physical features and that "not much more is needed to establish a great place in the hearts and minds of the public."[15] Though what is naturally occurring is not always considered desirable (it took ninety-five miles of piping to transform Central Park from marshes and bogs to lakes and meadows), today's sites have been largely stripped of all such features; therefore, the challenge, according to

Hargreaves, is how to "create [good] bones where there are none."[16]

One way the firm achieves this is by acknowledging a site's past condition in a diversity of ways: in scale, by creating forms modeled on those previously on or near the site but rescaled to different sizes; temporally, by conserving select artifacts or commemorating events; materially, by reestablishing the presence of hydrological systems, without restoring their previous forms. Using all of these approaches, Hargreaves Associates challenges the notion of landscape design as the creation of places of respite and remove. Instead, it seeks to reintegrate dilapidated sites with the dynamics of their physical surroundings by horizontal extension (physical connectivity, such as extending the existing urban grid into the park so as to create a seamless connection rather than a distinction) as well as by vertical extension (conceptual connectivity; also known as the palimpsest of the geologic approach that draws on the past as a way to build a context for the project).

This latter approach has been particularly fruitful for Hargreaves Associates; conceptual excavations help sponsor heterogeneous conditions that cannot be obtained by defining context based only on what is physically visible (as with contextualism's nostalgia for the present). For example, the early noteworthy projects Candlestick Point Park (1985–91) and Byxbee Park (1988–91) were, respectively, a rubble heap and a sanitary landfill when the firm was commissioned to design them.[17] These sites did not fit the conception of Kevin Lynch's "imageable" or Jane Jacobs's walkable places. Hargreaves Associates took inspiration from the accretion of layers in order to build the ground for the projects. This included not only reconfiguring physical material but also making references to a site's condition at another time, such as the landforms inspired by Indian shell middens at Byxbee Park.[18] Similarly, dune morphology motivated the creation of sheltered areas at Candlestick Point Park and, later, at Crissy Field, both of which are windswept sites that had naturally occurring dunes prior to industrialization and militarization. Fluvial inspired forms are used in Guadalupe River Park, Louisville Waterfront Park, and the University of Cincinnati. If a designed landform is motivated by a natural formation, it is unrecognizable as such because its surface is materially distinct from its source and it is scaled to the human body, rather than to its naturally occurring size. An obvious example can be seen when the abstracted topography is adjacent to its natural counterpart, such as the river channel at Guadalupe River Park. The two forms share no visible characteristics at the experiential level. And, notably, no matter what the reference or source of inspiration, none of the constructed landforms appear as natural outgrowths of the site.

Though the forms themselves are conspicuous, the various *sources* that inspire them are not as decipherable as Hargreaves's early statements about the narrative nature of the firm's work suggest.[19] The references are lost in translation because of the dissimilarity between the original formal inspiration and its scaled application to the site, as seen in Guadalupe River Park. This process of transformation denies their status as mere symbolic representations (a stand-in or sign of the past), rendering them grounds without clear prescriptions for use. In other words, though the sources of these forms are likely to remain unknown to the park's users, taking inspiration from the site's previous layers provides the basis for new formal and spatial configurations, producing unique and peculiar experiences within each site. This is what makes the work both specific to its place (it is meaningful to those involved in making the park who understand the references) but also open because the forms are scaled to provide other spatial, experiential, and programmatic opportunities.

More recently, Hargreaves has suggested that users do not need to "decode" a landscape to enjoy it—they might appreciate its surfaces (for picnicking, games, etc.) more than they value the regional typologies that a designer uses to organize the landscape.[20] Nevertheless, he believes that legibility is a key characteristic of successful public spaces, which occurs when visitors can "decipher how the landscape reads within its context, and how it is special and different from other landscapes."[21] His use of the term "legibility" refers to the perception of that which is singular (in other words, unique), not single in its physical manifestation or in terms of how it is meant to be deciphered (that is, homogenous). This distinction is important, especially in regard to developments that seek to create a coherent identity for a place (the mythic community). As sociologist Bella Dicks notes, the "entrepreneurial city" is aimed at reviving towns and cities that were devastated by the loss of manufacturing, and are using symbolism to promote themselves, especially symbolism drawn from their industrial pasts.[22] Though this approach is not new, the idea of "place promotion" has become increasingly common since the 1980s as cities adjust to the loss of manufacturing

by using such strategies to instigate economic growth. Dicks notes that place promotion is thematically coherent, which helps create a "visitor space that will produce carefully sited pools of consumption."[23] This is in contrast to place as understood by Hargreaves, which is heterogeneous and complex. Both approaches draw on the past of a site or region, but the former does so in an attempt to

freeze its identity– to brand it—whereas the latter looks to extant and former conditions to inspire the creation of a diversity of environments in order to preclude one interpretation or use from dominating the design.

FIGURE 16. The small, mounded forms at Byxbee Park landfill were inspired by Indian shell middens. These miniaturized trash heaps, oriented toward the dominant wind direction, sit perched on the much larger topography of trash below, collapsing the temporal dimension that separates various cultures' detritus. These topographic features also operate in more obvious ways since their maximum heights are just below eye level. The mounds are seen against the distant mountains, collapsing the space of the site with the larger geology within which it is situated; and the mounds were also seen in relation to the garbage mounds of the adjacent landfill until it ceased operation in 2011. All four references within one formation speak to Hargreaves's interest in acknowledgment, rather than resemblance. Image courtesy of John Gollings.

FIGURE 17. Candlestick Point Park after completion when the arced landforms inspired by dune formations are clearly visible. Image courtesy of John Gollings.

REMNANTS AND FRAGMENTS

A DIFFERENT APPROACH to history is the conservation of relics from previous uses, which is a more direct form of acknowledgment. If the landform designs in the previous examples stimulate imagination and unscripted use, the maintenance of actual relics has more to do with stimulating a "memory" of what the place used to be.[24] For example, at Chattanooga Waterfront Park, there are several sites dispersed along the waterfront where artifacts of its former industry, such as blast furnace remnants, are kept. These artifacts do not dominate the design—as at Richard Haag's Gas Works Park or Peter Latz's park in Duisburg Nord, the latter of which preserves entire facilities reprogrammed as public space—but are icons within the landscape. As for these latter projects, Hargreaves asks at what point we, as a society, are better off creating public space through remediation of the land and new programs rather than keeping relics of our industrial past, relics that might contribute to romanticizing both the technology that created the site contamination and the eventual loss of entire livelihoods, a tendency that contributes to a "troubling celebration of the industrial sublime."[25] Another example of using remnants is Hargreaves Associates' use of detritus found at the Candlestick Point Park for site furniture. This is similar to the use of recycled material in several projects by Michael Van Valkenburgh Associates, such as reclaimed stone slabs used for bleachers at Brooklyn Bridge Park, New York; or Julie Bargmann's (D.I.R.T.) design for Urban Outfitters in Philadelphia, where concrete excavated during construction was reused as paving, the broken slabs scattered to leave gaps where trees and gravel fill create a texturally varied surface.

The uses of remnants in these examples are quite distinct from themed environments, and have much more to do with recycling than with ruins. The distinction between using remnants and constructing new fragments is crucial: the preservation of something extant (a remnant) is distinct from a design approach that seeks to construct a relationship to the past by building fragments, such as the building of ruins in picturesque gardens.[26] A fragment, whether made up of existing remnants or made with entirely new materials, is meant to convey something partial or unfinished. For instance, a more contemporary example of constructing fragments is the Wexner Center, where architect Peter Eisenman designed a piece of his building to resemble a previously destroyed structure, and located it adjacent to the original structure's foundation. The "folies" of Bernard Tschumi's Parc de la Villette (1983) are meant to operate the same way by using the forms of nearby structures as inspiration and recombining them in unfamiliar ways, or simply making them look like a kit of parts collaged together. Tschumi notes that the folies were a "combination and transformation . . . developed from an existing figurative element (an 1865 pavilion on the site)" and are "recombined through a series of per-

FIGURE 18. Guadalupe River Park model showing the braided landforms inspired by river flow. The primary river channel is the sliver with blue paper in the bottom of the image.

FIGURE 19. A view of the braided landforms as experienced in the landscape. They do not resemble river formations at this scale. Image courtesy of Richard D. Beebe.

FIGURE 20. Gas Works Park by Richard Haag (opened in 1975) contains remnants of the coal gasification plant. Image courtesy of Myra Kohn.

FIGURE 21. Wexner Center by Peter Eisenman (1983–89). Ohio State University, Columbus. The fragmented structure designed by Eisenman was inspired by the armory tower that previously existed on the site. Image courtesy of Phyllis A. Valentine.

mutations whose rules have nothing to do with those of classicism or modernism."[27] Though post-modernism and deconstruction as architectural styles, inspired respectively by historicism and post-structuralism, were ideologically opposed (and seen in the work of Graves, Venturi, et al., versus Eisenman and Tschumi), both utilized fragment as their modus operandi. As one architectural critic notes, fragments are associated with myth, memory, and the world of wholeness to which they no longer belong.[28] In these examples, fragments are something out of place or incomplete, and are meant to be deciphered as such.

In contrast, when a recreated fragment coincides with its original purpose, such as reintroducing habitat that was demolished for development, it is not meant to be a symbol of something or somewhere else (though attempts to restore landscapes to some presumably pure ecological state before modernization suffer from the same sentiment of loss and myth). A relevant example is the creation of a salt marsh at Crissy Field, located in San Francisco's Presidio, a National Historical Landmark. When Hargreaves Associates received the commission to redesign Crissy Field, its life as a dog lovers' promenade and surfers' paradise, and previous life as both salt marsh and military air base, represented conflicting desires by various interest groups, each of which wanted the park remade for its particular constituency. A total marsh restoration would have prevented inclusion of any reference to the airfield, which had been declared a national monument and

FIGURE 26. The Passage of the Trail of Tears at Chattanooga Waterfront Park descends almost forty feet into a pool that sits adjacent to the river. Cherokee artists created tablets (seen inset into the wall on the left). A text explaining each tablet is located in the center of the steps, between wet ground and dry ground. One of the texts can be seen as a triangular figure inset in the middle foreground of the image.

Even though it is the text, rather than form and material, that *explains* the historic events, the physical structure, detailing, and water are what create the experience of this place. One criticism of this project might be that the mood is too celebratory and playful given the gravity of what it is meant to signify. On the one hand, the cascading fountain attracts many people to the site who may not have otherwise experienced it and, in that sense, can be informative to a larger number of people. Hargreaves includes interactive fountains in many of his projects because he believes this is one of the most successful ways to entice people to use a space. This is a particularly appropriate response to sites in hot climates, such as Louisville or Chattanooga. On the other hand, the most memorable aspect of the project is a grand cascading stair of water in an urban space. Though the water it is meant to symbolize tears, no one would make this association without reading the text, nor does the loud cascade of flowing water evoke tears. Such an interactive space might leave one feeling contented or refreshed, rather than reflective. In fact, the popularity of the space as a pool led the city to add continuous railings along it, as well as a regrettable colored lighting scheme that further contributes to its reading as a festival place.

The lead artist, Bill Glass, said that the artists wanted the space to celebrate the Cherokee living culture and not be only a memorial to a tragic event.[36] The project certainly succeeds in this regard; nevertheless, the combination of public space, heritage, and the accommodation of large events is increasingly common and begs the question of the "clientele" for whom the space was conceived. The shift from industrial to entertainment and service economies has meant that cities pay close attention to how to draw people downtown. Heritage tourism is one of the fastest growing markets in which to do this. This can be seen as a positive development in terms of education, especially when the cultures represented are involved in the process, as in the case of the Cherokee artists at Chattanooga; it can also lead to commodification of public space, however, as retail and themed environments are increasingly geared primarily to visitors rather than residents.[37] Moreover, most public space is now funded and managed with a significant amount of private investment, calling into question its "public" status. It has been noted that we are creating a two-tier park system, and a "pay to play" mind-set where parks must produce their own revenue and are overseen by private nonprofit groups.[38] The resulting issues of representation—who is being represented and by whom, as well as who funds and controls public space—are essential to understand. The design must strive for a balance among special interest groups who argue in support of particular uses in the public meetings (surfers, dog walkers, etc.), private funding and operations that could potentially limit activities, and unknown, underrepresented, or future constituents. Though Hargreaves acknowledges that too much public input can lead to freezing a park in moments that may be inappropriate, he also notes the importance of programming—providing space for varied activities—geared to the diverse groups of people a particular park serves.[39]

It will be interesting to see how the Los Angeles State Historic Park fares relative to the issues raised above, especially because it marks multiple histories and cultures rather than a single event. This site is a place of contestation, with a long history leading back to the founding of Los Angeles in the eighteenth century.[40] Given that the site is designated a state historic park, the interpretive program is fundamental to its mission. The California State Parks Department produced a 105-page document entitled the *Interpretative Master Plan*, which calls for an overriding theme of "Connectivity," two primary themes under that umbrella titled "Flow of History" and "Environmental Justice," and a secondary theme of "Recreation."[41]

Hargreaves Associates won the competition for the Los Angeles State Historic Park (LASHP) in 2006. Stranded bands that form the basis of the original schematic design derive from the rail yards that previously existed on the site. Hargreaves Associates did not literally trace the rail lines or replace the train tracks, but used them to inspire the overall banded organization. These bands, which are paths and plazas lined with rows of trees, comprise different programmatic zones on two-thirds of the site and provide the framework by which the "interpretative" aspects of the project are interwoven. The interpretive elements of the park program include a series of themed gardens, as well as texts and media access points that are distributed throughout the park.[42] The location of the previous locomotive turntable-roundhouse is registered, in approximate size and location, as a performance stage–lawn area rather than as a reconstruction. In other words, Hargreaves Associates has avoided the reconstruction of fragments that were lost to various stages of development, which would result in a theme-park effect on the site. But with so much programming packed into a relatively small site, it will be interesting to see whether its mission to be a regional attraction overshadows the needs of local residents, who desperately need recreational space.

The potential downside is that the park will become an outdoor museum because of the extent to which it is being *curated*, forged out of a collectivity that is based on remembrance. Despite the vitality of the site's history of environmental and social struggle, the mandate that the park be "historic" will, one hopes, not outweigh the fact that it must remain open to the current and future desires of the neighboring population, who fought hard to maintain this as public land. Most recently, in 2000, the Friends of the Los Angeles River (FoLAR) and local neighborhood groups organized to form the Chinatown Yards Alliance, which led to a yearlong series of events and reports about this area.[43] These reports on the history of the site eventually led to its purchase by the State of California. While some members of the Chinatown Yards Alliance hoped for designated recreational areas to predominate, the State Parks and Recreation Commission asserts that "sports fields are not considered resource-based recreation because they do not support recreational activities that are dependent on the cultural resources . . . of the site"; rather, the commission's goal is to "protect and improve the site to meet the needs of the statewide population, not only those residents who live nearby."[44] The Center for Law in the Public Interest challenged this position based on the grounds that sports fields are in keeping with the mandate of environmental justice, given that some members of this underserved community who want sports fields are relatives or descendants of those whose history is to be codified in the site narrative.[45] In the end, there are no formally designated recreational fields (an approach also taken at Crissy Field), but there are areas that are large and open enough that informal recreation is possible.[46] The process undertaken thus far suggests the park will be well balanced in terms of its various users, as groups such as the Chinatown Yards Alliance have been involved throughout the park's formation; however, the park must be revenue generating, which creates a potential conflict between an ostensibly public place and the activities it can or cannot sponsor.[47] In any case, we may never be able to evaluate the efficacy of Hargreaves Associates' original design, as the state budget crisis has caused its proposal to be indefinitely shelved, and a thirteen-acre interim park was built.

CONCLUSION

Instead of the linearity of an unbroken chain there is a vertical system of correspondences, a projection in depth; instead of the cause-and-effect relationships of an evolution or development, a set of retroactive confiscations; instead of the singularity of an origin, a complex network of distinct and multiple elements.[48]
—CRAIG OWENS

AS THE IMAGES on the following pages show, the firm's overall approach engages different temporal-material axes simultaneously. Together these axes form an oblique slice through time that ties together past, present, and future. Hargreaves Associates' projects cannot be explained with simple or single diagrams because they are not formulated that way. This resistance to easy classification derives from the desire for expressed multiplicity in which Hargreaves seeks to surface the rich history of the ground. At times this tactic is used for formal innovation (Byxbee Park); other times it is used to express differences through stark adjacencies of materials and forms (Crissy Field); and other projects are more explicit about the history we are to understand through the experience, conveying information via text and image (Trail of Tears and LASHP). The failings of previous modernist master plans and the colonizing tendencies of private development should not mean recourse to "utopianisms of pro-

cess" where design specificity is avoided. Hargreaves acknowledges that large sites cannot be remade all at once if funding and maintenance are not available, and so areas must be left "unmade." Yet the unmade areas must be as strategically located as any other part of the project in order to achieve the "disparate forms and site conditions [that are] critical to long-lived complexity."[49] In other words, the problem is not with planning or master plans per se; rather, the problem is with the unified plan.[50]

The tactic of acknowledgment, rather than replication or resemblance, has enabled Hargreaves Associates to derive unique and varied ground conditions that can be explained relative to the history of the site, yet it is inevitably used to support a diversity of uses, experiences, and, it is hoped, users. Much of the firm's success in navigating public processes and multiple constituencies is due to its ability to ground the designs in each project's extensive properties—geographic, material, and historical—combining these aspects in unique ways that do not privilege one over others. An apt statement made about Crissy Field is that the park is itself a political document, due to its diversity.[51] This is a key statement, one that delineates the distinction between the notion of *consensus* and that of *collective*. Everyone can accept a familiar or benign design response, which is consensus by default because it doesn't challenge the status quo. The collective, on the other hand, suggests the possibility of alliance without agreement. The projects shown on the following pages offer compelling examples of how diverse interests and site conditions are not simply managed through the process of negotiating design, but are also manifest in the designs themselves.

CRISSY FIELD

CRISSY FIELD IS PART OF THE PRESIDIO, A former military installation at the northern edge of San Francisco that is now part of the National Park System. The Presidio became a U.S. Army outpost in 1846, having been under the control of Spain from 1776 to 1822 and Mexico from 1822 to 1846. It was designated a National Historic Landmark in 1962 yet remained under active military control until 1994, making it the oldest continuously operating military post in the United States. In 1989, as part of widespread base closures in the United States, the Presidio became part of the Golden Gate National Recreation Area, which comprises eighty thousand acres of northern California's coastline.

The one-hundred-acre area that is now Crissy Field remained a salt marsh until the 1915 Panama-Pacific International Exposition, when it was filled in to create a racetrack. The flatness of the landfill made it ideal for use as a grass airfield and it was regularly used as such from 1920 to 1936, attaining status with several important achievements in aviation history. Crissy Field's cultural importance, its recent transfer to the National Park Service, and its location amid a dense urban environment at the base of the Bay Bridge made for diverse constituents, each with specific demands as to how the site should be developed as a public park. Hargreaves Associates' design process began with mapping the site as it existed at key moments in its history. The maps were used to create a series of overlays, which allowed the design team to compare the size and extent of various historical landscapes and then combine them on one drawing, as if they occurred simultaneously. Coupled with perspective design sketches overlaid on existing site photos, the plan overlay drawings enabled the client and the public to understand that the large expanse and open spatiality of the design could support many recreational uses.

The result is a deceptively simple plan that provides space for a range of activities, including parking for five hundred cars (80 percent of which is grass); a launch point for boardsailing; a 1.3-mile-long promenade; the reintroduction of eighteen acres of salt marsh and twenty-two acres of beach and sand dunes; and "restoration" of the airfield in the form of a twenty-eight-acre large grass plinth, whose outline is derived from the 1915 exposition racetrack. Other elements include small, sheltered areas for picnicking made with landforms on the northwestern edge of the site, and a grid of cypress trees adjacent to undulating landforms along the southeastern edge of the park. Though the project is often referred to as a restoration, it is far from it in any straightforward sense. Instead, Hargreaves Associates' redesign of Crissy Field simultaneously brings together two very different notions of a shifting landscape: one that marks particular moments of human-induced site change over time, and another that allows natural processes to enact material change on the site.

FIGURE 27. The Presidio can be seen in the center of the photo. Crissy Field is at its northern edge; the rectangular figure of the Golden Gate Park (1870s) can be seen to the south. Image courtesy of the U.S. Geological Survey.

FIGURE 28. Image courtesy of the U.S. Geological Survey.

FIGURE 29. Image courtesy of the U.S. Geological Survey.

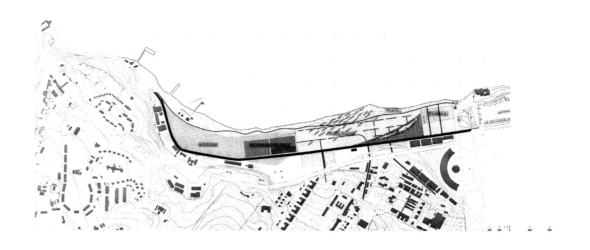

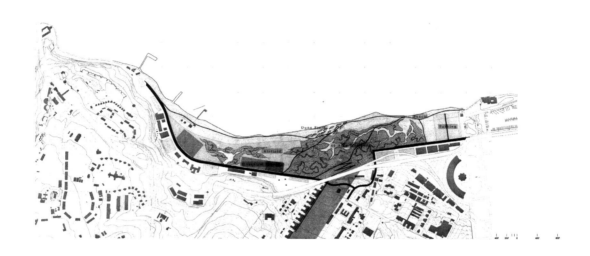

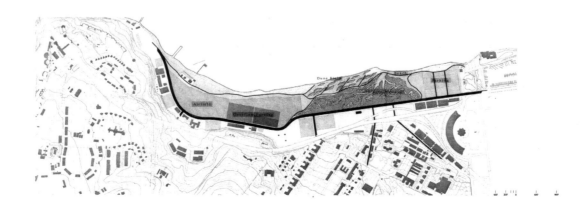

FIGURES 30-32. A series of overlay drawings of Crissy Field that considered a number of options for how the various program areas could relate to each other: "Stasis" does not include a marsh; "Palimpsest" overlaps the airfield and forty acres of marsh; and "Segmentation," which is the closest to the final plan, shows distinct areas abutting each other and includes a smaller marsh.

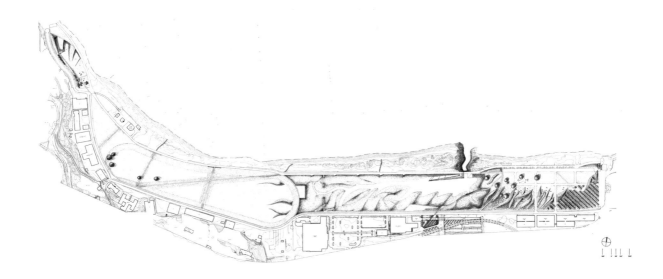

FIGURE 33. The plan (1998) of Crissy Field shows the various zones from west to east: the west bluff (top left of drawing) includes small, sheltered areas for picnicking made with landforms; the grass "airfield"; restored tidal wetlands and dunes; the east beach for large gathering, overflow parking, and launching area for windsurfers; all are connected with the promenade. An "orchard" of Monterey cypress trees and series of arced landforms mark the southeast entrance to the park. The trees were chosen to tie the flat expanse of Crissy Field into the larger Presidio given that the army had planted grids of cypress, pine, and eucalyptus throughout the Presidio in the late 1800s.

ABOVE

FIGURE 34. An aerial photograph (looking east) from 1921 showing the grass airfield. Image courtesy National Archives and Records Administration, Park Archives and Records Center, GOGA 2224, Crissy Field Study Collection, box 2, folder 2, neg. no. 20a.

TOP RIGHT

FIGURE 35. The large lawn plinth is graded along most of its northern edge to sit above the promenade, making an abrupt transition between the two zones. On the north side of the promenade (left in photo) there are restored dunes, protected with mesh fences to keep dogs and people out. Beyond the edge of the lawn plinth, and situated south of the promenade, is the marsh. ©Michael Macor / Corbis.

BOTTOM RIGHT

FIGURE 36. The promenade as it crosses the marsh inlet can be seen in the right of this photograph. Image courtesy of Ingrid Taylar.

FIGURE 38. The western, eastern, and southern edges of the marsh are also surrounded by dune vegetation (this photo is taken near Mason Street on the southeastern area of the park), which was planted by thousands of volunteers. Many of the plants were propagated from cuttings and seeds collected at the Presidio as well as those grown in the Presidio's own nursery because they are not readily available in commercial nurseries. Many mature Monterey cypress groves (seen on the right) occur throughout the park, creating shelter, though some people wanted them removed because they are not native. Image courtesy of Ken McCown.

FIGURE 39. The Tennessee River winds through downtown Chattanooga. The Hargreaves Associates project spans both sides of the river (seen in the center of the photo). Image courtesy of the U.S. Geological Survey.

FIGURE 40. Image courtesy of the U.S. Geological Survey.

FIGURE 41. Image courtesy of the U.S. Geological Survey.

FIGURE 42. Hargreaves Associates initiated this project with a series of small-scale clay models that show the topography at various points in the city's development. These were then photographed and overlaid with drawings of the streets and building fabric from the same dates as the topographic underlay. This process assists the designers' understanding of how the river's edge was transformed over time, and produces a general understanding of areas that were filled (shown in yellow). This image represents 1837.

FIGURE 43. The 1945 overlay shows that some streams were filled in and vegetation was removed.

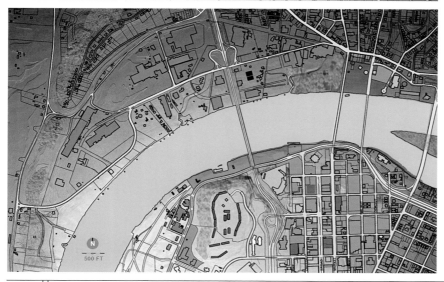

FIGURE 44. The 2002 overlay, when Hargreaves Associates and Schwartz Silver Architects were commissioned for the master planning effort.

THE NEW WATERFRONT HISTORICAL INTERPRETATION

Ross's Landing & Ferry
Trail of Tears
Bluff Furnace
Civil War
City's First Water Supply
Wharves & Riverboats
Bridges
Smokestack
City's first park
Moccasin Bend

—— Trail of Tears fragment
● interpretive site

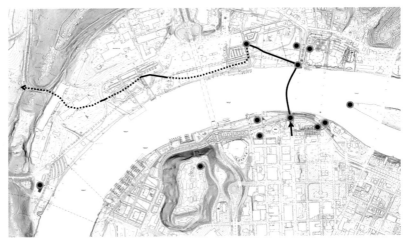

FIGURE 45. The design phase at Chattanooga Waterfront Park identified potential sites for historical interpretation. Blast furnace remnants were retained and, where no physical remnants remained, the design included interpretive clues, such as creating a forest clearing where the footprint of a former bridge existed.

FIGURE 46. The master plan, shown here overlaid on an aerial photograph, is divided into six primary districts: three on the north side and three on the south side of the Tennessee River. Three of the six districts—Ross's Landing, where the Trail of Tears is located (south side), the First Street Steps at the Bluff (south side), and Renaissance Park (north side)—contain thirty-nine acres of public space and were designed and built in just three years. All told, the master plan will have forty-six acres of mixed-use projects and eighty-three acres of open space, which includes the street upgrades and roadway realignment.

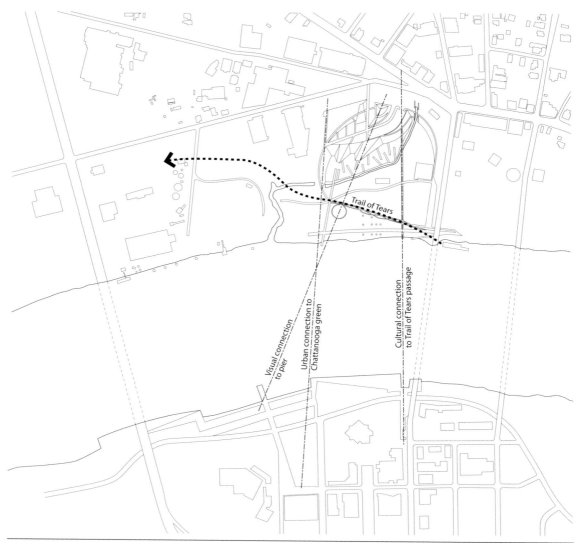

Trail of Tears

Visual connection to pier

Urban connection to Chattanooga green

Cultural connection to Trail of Tears passage

FIGURE 47. Hargreaves often begins by incorporating plan geometry from areas beyond a site's boundary. This precludes the park space from being perceived as bounded or distinct from the city and, in this case, uses the geometry to link both sides of the river. Redrawn by Keith VanDerSys based on information provided by Hargreaves Associates.

Existing forest

Urban/ disturbed

Acer negundo (temporarily flooded forest alliance)

Robinia pseudoacacia (forest alliance)

Albizia julibrissins (forest alliance)

Market St. branch (appx. 475 acre watershed)

Old stream bed

Fault lines

FIGURE 48. The design of Renaissance Park had to take into account numerous surface and subsurface conditions that helped guide plan organization. This image shows the design overlaid with the existing forest and streambed that empties into the Tennessee River. The constructed wetland is located north of this stream (where the old streambed used to be) and intercepts and circulates the stormwater before releasing it back into the stream. Redrawn by Keith VanDerSys based on information provided by Hargreaves Associates.

Legend:
- 1930+
- Groundwater contaminants
- Capped waste cells (enamel frit)
- + 50% fill (scrap metal, rubble)
- Seeps

industrial plan (stamping + plating post-1926)

remediation area 1960's- 1970's

FIGURE 49. This drawing overlays Hargreaves Associates' design with a contamination map showing both soil and groundwater contamination. The arrows show seeps, where contaminants entered frit ponds for capturing the by-product of the enameling process that previously occurred here. This area was improperly remediated in the 1960s and 1970s: it was capped but no liner was placed underneath it to prevent seepage into the groundwater. The design excavated the contaminated soils from this area, located the new constructed wetland over it, and capped the soils within landforms that were built on higher ground and out of the groundwater and floodplain zone. Redrawn by Keith VanDerSys based on information provided by Hargreaves Associates.

FIGURE 50. A view from the south side of the river looking north. The walkway overhang on the north side of the river at Renaissance Park aligns with the Trail of Tears Passage across from it. The large hill beyond, which caps the landfill, is a favorite spot for grass sledding. Image courtesy of Lawrence G. Miller.

FIGURE 51. The Waterfront Park on the south shore of the Tennessee River is a narrow sliver of land between the Parkway (roadway) and the river. Faceted planes lead pedestrians to the river's edge. Image courtesy of Lawrence G. Miller.

FIGURE 52. A similar language of faceted planes is used at Renaissance Park to frame the constructed wetland that captures stormwater prior to its release into the Tennessee River. The capped landfill can be seen in the background. Image courtesy of John Gollings.

LOS ANGELES STATE HISTORIC PARK (2006–2008 SCHEMATIC DESIGN PHASE)

THE LOS ANGELES STATE HISTORIC PARK IS located adjacent to downtown, just south of the confluence of the Los Angeles River and the Arroyo Seco. The site sits at the foot of Elysian Park, Los Angeles's oldest and second-largest park. The 1930 Olmsted-Bartholomew plan for the Los Angeles region recommended that the entire area around Elysian Park and the Chavez Ravine— where Dodger Stadium was built in the 1950s—be obtained for what they called "regional athletic fields," envisioned as large, flat areas of at least one hundred acres. The plan also called for a vehicular parkway running along the Arroyo Seco and for the surrounding fourteen hundred acres of land to be protected as public parks. The Olmsted-Bartholomew plan was not adopted by the city. Though the Arroyo Seco Parkway (Pasadena Freeway) was built in 1940, it was done so without the associated public space. Rather than use the flood zone for recreation, the Army Corps of Engineers encased both the Los Angeles River and the Arroyo Seco in concrete channels.

Recent efforts to make both rivers accessible for public use include the newly adopted Los Angeles River Revitalization Master Plan (2005–7), a fifty-one-mile greenway that will connect the San Gabriel Mountains to the Pacific Ocean. The LASHP site, while it comprises only thirty-two acres, provides an important link along the corridor, since its northeastern edge adjoins the Los Angeles River channel, its west edge abuts Chinatown, and it will bridge to Elysian Park. As with most contemporary landscape projects, it involves knitting together

FIGURE 53. The Los Angeles State Historic Park site
(the tan-colored fish-shaped wedge) can be seen to the
southeast of Dodger Stadium. Image courtesy of the U. S.
Geological Survey.

connections that were severed over decades of growth. Thus, Hargreaves Associates' submittal for the competition phase of the project focused on these larger connections to situate the site within the context of Elysian Park and the Los Angeles River. The proposal emphasizes four large-scale strategies, three of which the firm terms "biodiversity" strategies: connectivity, hydrology, and vegetation communities. The fourth strategy reconsiders the programmatic distribution in Elysian Park in order to consolidate high-activity areas.

These large-scale strategies are also used at the site scale, where they take on explicit thematic content so as to call out differences in cultural definitions of nature. This is evident in the pathways and gardens. For example, the Slope Garden running along the community pathway uses plants to illustrate changing aesthetic tastes: from plants that would have been common to the area prior to the region's explosive growth to a subsequent preference for Mediterranean and, later, subtropical plants, and the presumably future preference for drought-tolerant plants that are not necessarily locally native but are well suited to the climate and reflect a growing awareness of the need to restrict water use.

The pathways have recurring themes. For example, the community pathway, as noted above, refers to water use via vegetation, but there is also a pathway dedicated to "Water" that will convey information about water use from early settlement to a proposed wetland, and a "Nature" pathway focuses on the Los Angeles River and the proposed wetland. The Nature and Water pathways overlap

FIGURE 54. Image courtesy of the U.S. Geological Survey.

in one of the Second Nature gardens, whose vegetation is themed according to early settlement and agriculture. The result is a plan with layered and intersecting time lines, rather than something distinctly zoned, as at Crissy Field. This leads to some odd distinctions, such as isolating Nature, Culture, and Water as distinct themes, but it also allows for overlapping readings of environmental transformation. In other words, the fact that the resultant plan does not make clear hierarchical distinctions may well be the point given its mission to represent the history and diversity of multiple cultures.

FIGURE 55. Image courtesy of the U.S. Geological Survey.

FIGURE 56. The site can be seen (center left) at the foot
of Elysian Park. The channelized Los Angeles River can be
seen in the foreground. As of this writing, it is unknown if
Hargreaves's scheme will be constructed. There is currently
an interim park on the site, as seen in this photo with Lauren
Bon's Anabolic Monument (2009) in the foreground. Aerial
photograph by Joshua White. ©2009 Metabolic Studio.

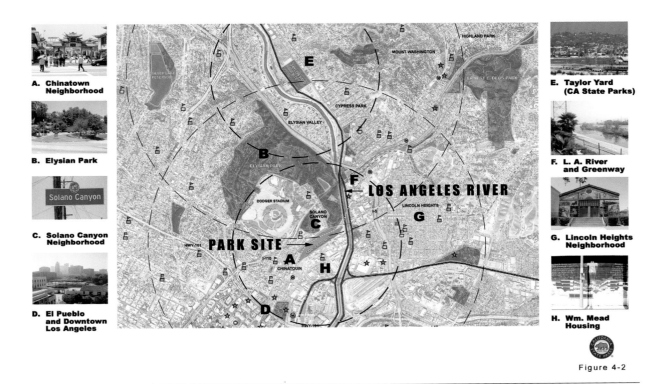

A. Chinatown Neighborhood

B. Elysian Park

C. Solano Canyon Neighborhood

D. El Pueblo and Downtown Los Angeles

E. Taylor Yard (CA State Parks)

F. L. A. River and Greenway

G. Lincoln Heights Neighborhood

H. Wm. Mead Housing

Figure 4-2

FIGURE 57. This Regional Connectivity drawing shows the thirty-two-acre site with respect to adjacent neighborhoods and parks and its proximity to the Los Angeles River. Image cropped from *Los Angeles State Historic Park, Regional Connectivity (Cornfield Site), General Plan and Final Environmental Impact Report*, Figure 4-2. Image © 2005, California State Parks.

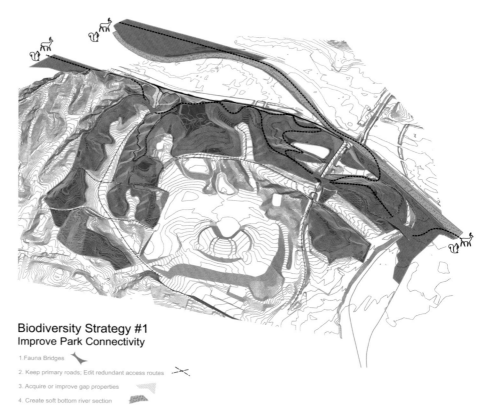

Biodiversity Strategy #1
Improve Park Connectivity

1. Fauna Bridges
2. Keep primary roads; Edit redundant access routes
3. Acquire or improve gap properties
4. Create soft bottom river section

TOP

FIGURE 58. The first biodiversity strategy—connectivity—recommends building bridges to enable wildlife crossings, removing excess roads to improve continuity of habitat, and acquiring additional patches of property.

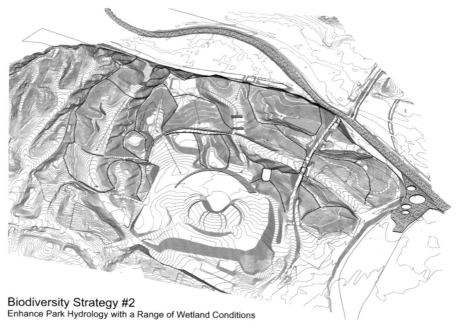

Biodiversity Strategy #2
Enhance Park Hydrology with a Range of Wetland Conditions

1. Ephemeral: stormwater wetlands
2. Perrenial: drainage wetlands along ridges
3. Floodplain: riparian condition at LA river
4. Future restoration of LA river

BOTTOM

FIGURE 59. The second biodiversity strategy recommends building a range of wetland conditions that capture and filter stormwater, as well as tie into the future Los Angeles River revitalization plan.

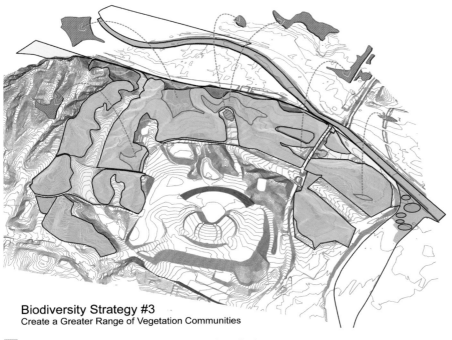

Biodiversity Strategy #3
Create a Greater Range of Vegetation Communities

1. Restore non-turf slopes to scrub / shrub / chaparral or grassland. Remove invasives.

2. Restore Walnut Forest

3. Create Hydrological conditions that connect patches

4. Remove turf at high elevations. Replace playing fields at Cornfield and Dodger Stadium

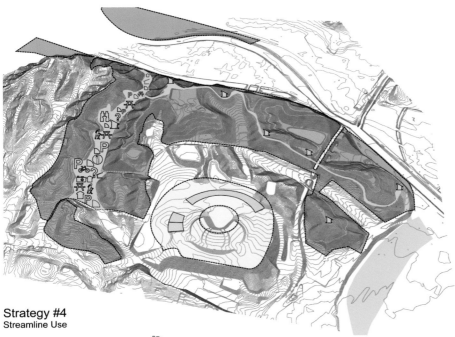

Strategy #4
Streamline Use

1. Stadium Way: park program

2. Doger's Stadium outer lots: multiple use

3. Ridgeline Trail: service points

FIGURE 60. The third biodiversity strategy proposes the removal of large areas of turf by reestablishing the native scrub vegetation and adding forest cover.

FIGURE 61. The fourth strategy consolidates the program into two areas: the western side of Elysian Park and the LASHP, connecting the two areas with a pathway along the ridge. This would result in a contrast between areas of dense activity surrounded by less intensely used areas. Additionally, Hargreaves proposed that the often unused Dodger Stadium parking lot be reconfigured for public recreation on non-game days.

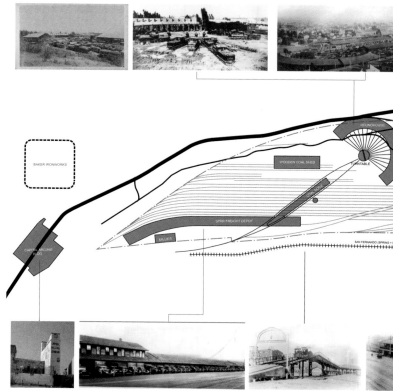

BAKER IRONWORKS

ROUNDHOUSE

WOODEN COAL SHED

TURNTABLE

SP RR FREIGHT DEPOT

MILLIE'S

CAPITAL MILLING CO.

SAN FERNANDO (SPRING + B...

FIGURE 62. The site was used by Southern Pacific Rail for 120 years, which enabled the transport of goods and the influx of people to Los Angeles. This site was the terminus of one of the transcontinental rail lines. Southern Pacific railroad yard, aerial view, 1924, Los Angeles Public Library, file # G-000-204; file: Transportation—Railroads—Southern.

FIGURE 63. This drawing shows the layout of the site when it was used by Southern Pacific Rail. The stranded bands of train tracks and turntable provided inspiration for Hargreaves Associates' plan organization. Plan drawing courtesy of Hargreaves Associates. Photographs are from various sources: top left courtesy the W. H. Fletcher Collection: Los Angeles Co.: Los Angeles: Railroads: Southern Pacific Roundhouse, call number: 1989-0527, neg. # 28,322, control number: 1379480; top second from the right courtesy the William Reagh Collection: Los Angeles Co.: Los Angeles: Railroads: View 2 of 2, call number: 1990-1541, neg. # 27,980 (4 x 5 in.), control number: 1382990.

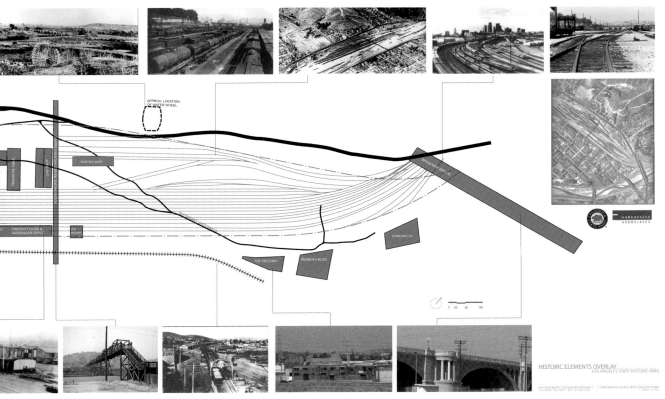

INTERPRETIVE PATHS AND PORTALS

Interpretive elements: shade structure with words/images, storytelling space, words embedded in paths, tabletop

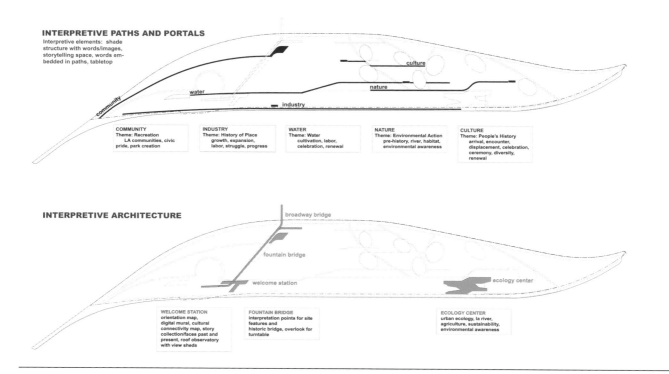

COMMUNITY
Theme: Recreation
LA communities, civic pride, park creation

INDUSTRY
Theme: History of Place
growth, expansion, labor, struggle, progress

WATER
Theme: Water
cultivation, labor, celebration, renewal

NATURE
Theme: Environmental Action
pre-history, river, habitat, environmental awareness

CULTURE
Theme: People's History
arrival, encounter, displacement, celebration, ceremony, diversity, renewal

INTERPRETIVE ARCHITECTURE

broadway bridge

fountain bridge

welcome station

ecology center

WELCOME STATION
orientation map, digital mural, cultural connectivity map, story collection/faces past and present, roof observatory with view sheds

FOUNTAIN BRIDGE
interpretation points for site features and historic bridge, overlook for turntable

ECOLOGY CENTER
urban ecology, la river, agriculture, sustainability, environmental awareness

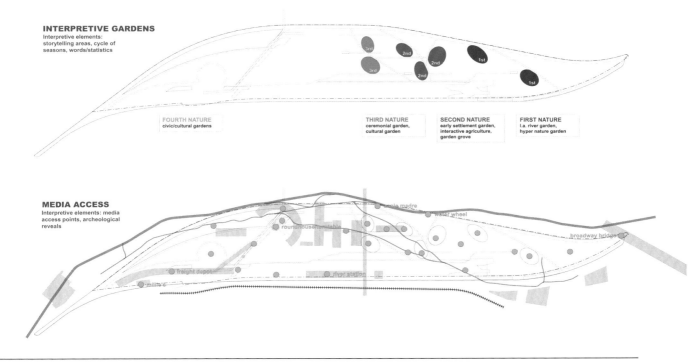

INTERPRETIVE GARDENS
Interpretive elements:
storytelling areas, cycle of
seasons, words/statistics

FOURTH NATURE
civic/cultural gardens

THIRD NATURE
ceremonial garden,
cultural garden

SECOND NATURE
early settlement garden,
interactive agriculture,
garden grove

FIRST NATURE
i.a. river garden,
hyper nature garden

MEDIA ACCESS
Interpretive elements: media
access points, archeological
reveals

FIGURE 64. These drawings show the "interpretative" layers
of the project. The five primary pathways (top left diagram)
run lengthwise across the site. The building and bridge
structures are concentrated in two areas and provide access
to fountains and wetlands. Interpretive gardens are nestled
among a secondary path system. The gardens are arranged
according to different "natures": the first three drawn
from John Dixon Hunt's explication of the three natures,
and a fourth nature, located at the entry plaza along the
southwestern edge of park, that pertains to environmental
justice and past struggles over land use. In addition, media
access points are scattered throughout the park.

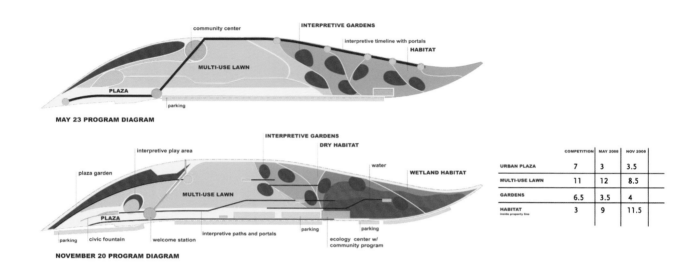

community center

INTERPRETIVE GARDENS

interpretive timeline with portals

HABITAT

MULTI-USE LAWN

PLAZA

parking

MAY 23 PROGRAM DIAGRAM

INTERPRETIVE GARDENS

DRY HABITAT

interpretive play area

water

WETLAND HABITAT

plaza garden

MULTI-USE LAWN

PLAZA

parking   civic fountain   welcome station   interpretive paths and portals   parking   parking

ecology center w/
community program

NOVEMBER 20 PROGRAM DIAGRAM

	COMPETITION	MAY 2008	NOV 2008
URBAN PLAZA	7	3	3.5
MULTI-USE LAWN	11	12	8.5
GARDENS	6.5	3.5	4
HABITAT inside property line	3	9	11.5

FIGURE 65. As the project developed, the percentages of area given to particular programs changed. The area designated as "habitat" zones increased almost fourfold from the competition submittal, emphasizing the natural habitat component of the site's history.

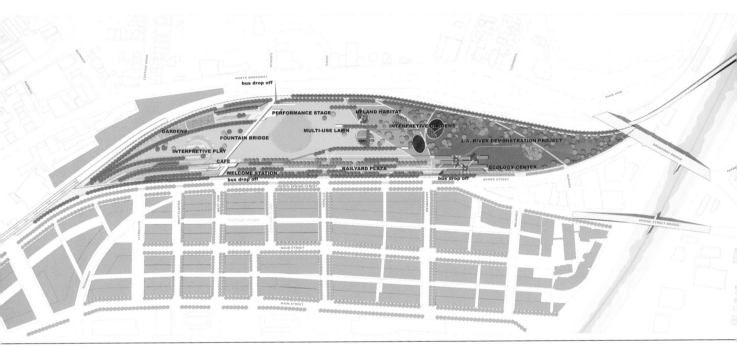

FIGURE 66. The competition entry had the interpretative program of history and ecology encircling an "activity field" that comprised one-third of the site. Changes made since then (seen in this plan) show a multiuse field with a large sloping lawn figure within it, facing onto a small stage that marks the location of the former rail turntable. This inclined plane somewhat divides the area designated as multiuse lawn into smaller, peripheral spaces so there is less flat open (flexible) space.

FIGURE 68. The wetland, seen after reconfiguration, sits at the terminus of Olympic Boulevard. The pyramidal mound can be seen on the right of it, and Haslams Creek, which receives water from the wetland, can be seen in the foreground. Image courtesy of John Gollings.

An extensive series of wetlands, intended to educate the public about issues of water management, while remediating the site and accommodating recreational uses, is also part of the 114-acre Brightwater Wastewater Treatment Plant in Snohomish County, Washington.[19] Seventy acres were a former auto salvage yard and contain the treatment plant facilities, while the 40 acres that sit just north of this area are restored habitat, a process that included uncovering approximately fourteen hundred linear feet of streams that had been buried in pipes. Existing wetlands were repaired and new ones built in order to improve water quality and habitat. Public access, habitat improvement, and education (with facilities and placards) were among the mitigations that were negotiated to convince nearby residents to agree to this location for the treatment plant.[20] Thus the landscape is required to play an overtly didactic role. This project is not the first to combine a public park with a wastewater treatment plant, but it is unique in that it is attempting to create a destination out of it. Other examples with parks in proximity to wastewater treatment plants tend to hide the facility itself behind large planted walls, in the case of Washington's West Point Treatment Plant, or to literally stack a landscape on top of it, as in New York City's North River Water Pollution Control Plant, which is covered by a 28-acre state park.[21] Visitors are likely unaware of what is going on because of the camouflage; in fact, this aspect is celebrated by the landscape architects of the North River plant, who note that it is designed so that "the resulting appearance is that of an on-grade environment," meaning that visitors may not know they are on top of a building

(since access is from above), let alone a sewage plant.[22] The fact that Hargreaves and the Brightwater client decided early that they would celebrate the treatment process signifies an important change in how this type of infrastructure can be integrated with publicly accessible landscapes.

The reality is that the wastewater that is treated within the buildings and tanks at Brightwater does not enter the site's landscape.[23] Rather, it is the stormwater circuit—that which captures rainwater that falls on the site and rooftops—that is a primary expressive structure used to promote the project. The two systems remain separate as far as input and output but, according to the mitigation manager, "Finding a way to fix a problem of stormwater runoff overwhelming [adjacent] Little Bear Creek was a major selling point of the project."[24] This is similar to the strategy used at Sydney Olympic Park, in that the cycles are kept physically separate but are conceptually and spatially linked. And, like at Sydney, though the soil profiles and water flow volumes are carefully controlled, the wetland figures at Brightwater vary from long, narrow rectangles to crescent- and bean-shaped ponds. The multiple forms and planting strategies on display as one circulates through the landscape frame the relationships among the stable and organic, fluid aspects of the landscape in different ways. This results in adjoining contrasting environments wherein clear lines of demarcation register different maintenance regimes, or where wetlands and forests abut manicured areas or patently constructed topography. What is apparent in Hargreaves Associates' approach is that different artifacts or systems can perform similarly in measurable ways without appearing identical. There is never one answer to a specific criterion, and in this choice of form lie the symbolic, aesthetic, and subjective aspects of function.

FLOW

THERE IS NO BETTER example of the contradiction between various definitions of function (and the supposedly optimal form to supply that function) than the channelization of rivers. Increased urban development has not only affected water quality because of polluted runoff, but it has also increased water quantity flowing into our streams and rivers. The more impervious surface there is, the greater the stress on the waterways that remain. Though constructed wetlands and underground storage help reduce the load on rivers and streams, rivers will inevitably overflow the channels that we construct to contain them.

A comparison of diverse proposals for the Guadalupe River Park in San Jose, California, in a series spanning three decades (1969–2002), provides a clear indication of how different assumptions about function affect a river. In 1989 Hargreaves Associates created the fifth of six different plans produced during this period, and almost two-thirds of the downtown river reconstruction in existence today was built according to the firm's design. Three earlier proposals are particularly germane to this issue, manifesting divergent conceptions about urban rivers in comparison to Hargreaves Associates' proposal: the first master plan created by Lawrence Halprin (1969), and the two immediately preceding Hargreaves Associates' plan, designed by the United States Army Corp of Engineers (early 1980s, which dealt primarily with flood volumes) and by EDAW (1983–85, which happened concurrently but dealt primarily with the recreational-park aspects). The fact that each proposal was overwritten by a subsequent scheme illustrates the changing cultural, political, and financial contexts within which the river was reconfigured. Moreover, the fact that Hargreaves Associates' proposal was itself challenged and, in the end, a large segment of it not built according to the firm's design exemplifies the contested nature of such projects.[25]

A total of 14.8 miles of the Guadalupe River has undergone or is still undergoing renovation, a process initially made financially possible by the Water Resources Development Act (1986).[26] The portion that concerns Hargreaves Associates' work is a segment over two and a half miles in length that runs through downtown San Jose, a tangle of infrastructure including the river channel, utilities, surface streets, and freeways that span across it. Hargreaves Associates was hired to develop alternatives to the United States Army Corps of Engineers (US-ACE) proposal, which would have made this stretch of the Guadalupe River largely inaccessible, while still meeting the USACE requirement to double the hydraulic capacity of the river.[27] Hargreaves Associates was able to combine recreational use with flood control, while eliminating other water controls called for in the Halprin and EDAW plans.

Halprin's scheme predated the USACE flood-control plan. It incorporated several lakes and a lagoon with program elements such as a boathouse and amphitheater. EDAW's proposal included provisions for flood control, but it also required that the natural water supply be supplemented to fill a series of lakes to maintain these constant water bodies for recreational use.[28] In other words, both Halprin and EDAW conceived of the site as being formed by the presence of water and programmed their schemes accordingly; both schemes absorb the river flow into static water bodies.[29] The relatively low frequency and quantity of precipitation in this area (averaging fifteen inches per year) meant that supplemental water would be required to fulfill the aesthetic and programmatic objectives of either of these plans, for which a series of dams would be necessary to create the lakes and lagoon. Hargreaves Associates, on the other hand, conceived of the river in terms of the absence of water. The design accepts dryness as much as it accepts flooding. The scheme does not use water to supplement the channel, and it does not include any lakes or ponds.[30] In the area where both Halprin and EDAW envisioned a lake, Hargreaves Associates proposed a flood meadow—a multiuse field that could be inundated

during heavy winter rains and used for events when dry.[31]

Hargreaves Associates' scheme expresses a striated ground. In the upper (southern) half of the project the channel is constructed in layers; a low-flow channel for fish passage sits within the concrete mattresses at the channel bottom that collect sediment and foster plant growth. The lower zones of retaining walls are made with stepped gabions (porous, rock-filled cages), whereas the higher portions of the walls are composed of stone and concrete terraces. The two zones are planted with different species. Within the gabions, additional vegetation collects; within the concrete and stone terraces, vegetation is planted and irrigated. The contrast between colonized versus planted, and unirrigated versus irrigated, is apparent in the resulting vertical banding. The upper stratum of hard material provides a datum against which the more porous bottom layers are seen in flux. In this stretch, the circulation of water and people are stacked in close proximity.

OPPOSITE, TOP TO BOTTOM

FIGURE 69. Lawrence Halprin's schematic plan for "Park of the Guadalupe" includes several lakes with meandering edges and program elements such as a boathouse and amphitheater. The plan proposes other commercial development in groupings of buildings and kiosks, figured to create a series of interlocking courtyards and terraces. Process infiltrates Halprin's language and drawings, but it has multiple meanings and expressions. Halprin's approach to the Guadalupe River Park is similar to his Portland and Seattle projects—formed as immersive "interiors"—rather than his Sea Ranch project (Sonoma County, 1961–67), which was left rougher, less manicured, and less controlled. (North is to the bottom right.) Image from the Lawrence Halprin Collection, the Architectural Archives, University of Pennsylvania.

FIGURE 70. EDAW (partial plan shown here) proposed different character zones that would correspond to, and help define, the surrounding program (zones A–F move south to north in the direction of flow, which is from left to right in this image). Image courtesy of the City of San Jose.

FIGURE 71. Though the Hargreaves Associates plan maintained the zoning from the EDAW plan, the firm proposed undulating terraces best for water flow (whereas Halprin's and EDAW's geometries are faceted) along much of zones A–C and E. For zone D, where both Halprin and EDAW proposed a lake, Hargreaves proposed a flood meadow—a multiuse field that could be inundated during heavy winter rains and used for events when dry. Hargreaves Associates' scheme does not use water to supplement the channel itself; there are no lakes or ponds. (North is to the bottom right.)

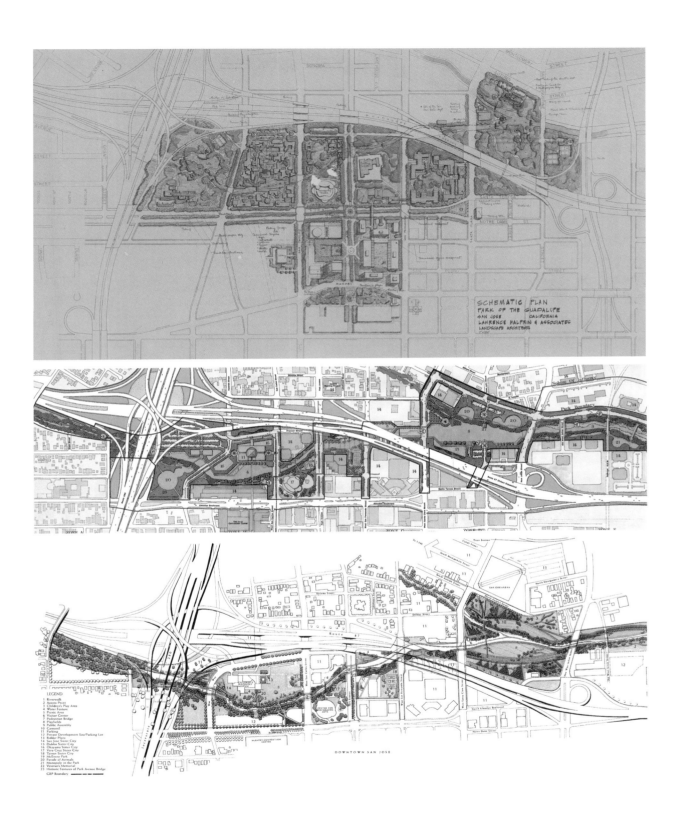

LEGEND
1 Riverwalk
2 Access Point
3 Children's Play Area
4 Water Feature
5 Picnic Area
6 Visitor Center
7 Pedestrian Bridge
8 Playfields
9 Public Assembly
10 Carousel
11 Parking
12 Private Development Site/Parking Lot
13 Ridder Plaza
14 San Jose Sister City
15 Dublin Sister City
16 Okayama Sister City
17 Vera Cruz Sister City
18 Tainan Sister City
19 McEnery Park
20 Parade of Animals
21 Monopoly in the Park
22 Veteran's Memorial
23 Historic Features of Park Avenue Bridge
        GRP Boundary

DOWNTOWN SAN JOSE

In contrast, the downstream area has more room for the water flow to spread and was made without reinforcing walls or terraces (except where it was already encased at the property boundary). The water itself is not easily visible or accessed; it is lined with existing, dense vegetation and the pedestrian circulation route remains well out of view of the water during most of the year, even though it (i.e., the route) is within the flood zone. This area is made with a series of landforms interwoven with pathways. In contrast to the upper reach, where vertical layering is achieved with contrasting material, the downstream area achieves layering perspectivally, depending on one's vantage point; as the landforms recede in the distance, they create a rhythm of light and dark, high and low. Thus, the strategy for the upper reach can be thought of as *exposing* the river processes, whereas the downstream zone is one of *expressing* the river processes. The change in material and form is based on this distinction. Both zones are open to fluctuation, yet the techniques for exposing, expressing, and controlling water are different, resulting in very distinct experiences of the river.

Though Hargreaves has not positioned his work directly in relation to recent ecological theories, the conception of landscapes as dynamic and open to disturbance, rather than in stasis, is an appropriate way to characterize Hargreaves Associates' scheme compared to the other schemes mentioned above.[32] Because the water level is not maintained at a consistent height through supplementary water and pumps, pockets of vegetation colonize some areas and are washed away in others. Even so, the freedom of the river is a largely symbolic but important gesture. In actuality, the Guadalupe River is

a channelized river. Irrespective of whether it is constrained within a USACE concrete channel or a Hargreaves Associates gabion-concrete-earthen retained channel, the river is not free to meander or change course. Both are technological or infrastructural systems, yet they use different techniques to construct the system: planar straight walls compared with stepped curvilinear walls, a single material versus a variety of materials, circulation of water compared with circulation of water *and* people, monotechnic versus polytechnic. Both the Hargreaves Associates and USACE schemes would perform the requisite flood control and meet the same quantifiable energy inputs and outputs; thus they look as they do by choice, not by need. And while the earlier schemes by EDAW and Halprin convey a greater image of control than does Hargreaves Associates' design, each project requires the same amount of detailing, engineering, and modeling, though the Hargreaves Associates proposal would likely use less energy to maintain because it is less controlled.

The belief that sustainability measures, ecology, and engineering simply work with quantifiable functions like flood control (energy inputs and outputs) is doubly problematic.[33] On the one hand is the implication that form and aesthetics are simply taken care of when one emphasizes quantifiable measures. This belief—that there is an ideal or predetermined form, or that form simply follows function—precludes the notion that functional requirements can steer formal and aesthetic agendas in specific ways. And on the opposite hand is the presumption that the pragmatic aspects of landscape are accommodated within the formal and aesthetic agendas, without being inherently political, which presumes that we can all agree on quantifiable, "objective" matters. Neither view is practicable when building public landscapes, where different ideologies are at play in terms of how landscape function is defined or understood.

Various quantifiable criteria—whether for protecting people, property, or fish—are often at odds with each other. Nowhere is this more evident than in the process that occurred during the building of Guadalupe River Park. In the end, Hargreaves Associates' project was halted after it was only half constructed. Though the channel met the criteria for flood flows, conservation groups objected to the proposal based on the project's certification under the Clean Water Act, which includes measures to protect wildlife, namely salmon habitat.[34] The area in question was a portion of the project that had existing riparian vegetation that would have been removed to widen the channel to meet the required flood volumes. Construction was stopped for three years until the parties reached agreement over a redesign. In the end, an underground bypass was created to redirect flood water, dumping it downstream, and leaving the existing vegetation intact. At this point, yet another firm was hired (Sasaki Associates) to design new inlet and outlet structures; the inlet culvert was placed where Hargreaves Associates had located the flood meadow. An important question to ask when it comes to landscape construction is: when does the end result (in this case it would have been a wider channel and eventually more planting) justify the means of temporary disturbance? At the very least, it is important to distinguish between conservation (protecting large areas of intact habitat) and reconstructing connectivity through our highly urbanized environments (as in downtown San Jose), where construction might be detrimental in the short term but result in a more robust long-term environment for people and wildlife.[35]

As the Guadalupe River Park project illustrates, there is no agreement as to what makes a landscape sustainable or ecological, though both terms permeate any discussion of design today. Nor do we know if individual best-management practices for handling stormwater are entirely beneficial; many of these techniques are still experimental, as in the case of wetlands for capturing stormwater.[36] For example, even if human contact is limited, which is unlikely, the degree of risk to wildlife using wetlands that filter urban runoff is still unknown. In other words, there are potential conflicts between water quality and habitat goals.[37] Because of these potential conflicts, how success is determined and quantified depends on which type of function is privileged.

RESISTANCE

WHAT IS CLEAR from the comparison among Hargreaves Associates projects is that the firm does not presume that site functions look a certain way or that sustainability refers only to quantifiable measures. And though some might criticize the firm for not adhering to a consistent set of principles, these projects are widely varied in the human activity they are designed to support. What is consistent is that, even within individual projects, Hargreaves Associates employs a range of techniques and varied degrees of control so as to prompt an awareness of

FIGURE 72. The North 40 area of Brightwater Wastewater Treatment Plant soon after construction, showing one of the reconstructed streams flowing into a pond.

the constructed essence of our environment. This is especially true with regard to how Hargreaves Associates creates topography as resistive form, both physically (in site stabilization) and expressively (in avoiding natural-looking landscapes).

The quantifiable factors that pertain to soil—its structural limitations or level of contamination—are folded into the detailing and construction of the projects in order to foster a specific design agenda, which is to transform flat, cleared sites into topographically diverse landscapes that have experiential range, and to do so in a way that provokes the sense that these landscapes are not merely fragments of preserved nature. The construction techniques used

for making many of the landforms in Hargreaves Associates' work are designed to resist the forces that would otherwise erode those landforms. Some of these landforms are made from contaminated material that is sealed within them, an approach that has been criticized for masking what hides beneath.[38] Also unseen are the engineered substrates (special gravel mixtures, fabrics, and plastic cells that enable the shaping of the topography), which are used to stabilize the ground structurally (so it doesn't sink or slide) and surficially (so it doesn't erode).

At Brightwater, the massive earthen structures range from heights of twenty feet to over sixty feet above the existing elevation. Many landforms that are triangular or trapezoidal in profile are reinforced at their edges with subsurface geocells (three-dimensional grid structures filled with gravel) in order to maintain a sharp profile and stable lines of transition between the turf-topped landforms and their sloped sides.[39] These stabilization techniques allow Hargreaves Associates to push the limits of the size and profile of the ground, and are used adjacent to areas that are prone to fluctuation. The contrast between the pyramidal mound and wetland at Sydney Olympic Park and the elaborate range of landforms intended for Parque do Tejo e Trancao in Lisbon demonstrate an obvious desire to resist naturalization in the appearance of the landscape by framing the fluid and cyclical materials within a visibly controlled, formal structure.

Advances in technology (such as software that enables greater accuracy for balancing cut and fill material on site and the use of global positioning systems to guide earth-moving equipment in the field) have helped Hargreaves Associates maintain precision in its earthworks as the projects have gotten bigger and more complex. Even so, for a project as large as Brightwater, which required excavation of almost one million cubic yards of material, exact soil quantities cannot be known in advance. Nevertheless, Hargreaves Associates details its projects in order to maintain precision of form. The two largest hills in Brightwater were designed with a predetermined profile and shape, but with their final size unknown. Hargreaves Associates designed the minimum and maximum profiles for each hill, and anything beyond the maximum will go into an adjacent flat plinth. The firm's design and detailing maintain a *defined set of relationships* where the vari-

able amount of material unearthed during construction is applied within the constraints of predetermined forms. In other words, the indeterminacy of material is not exclusive of formal precision.

CONCLUSION

THROUGHOUT THE HISTORY of the discipline, landscape architects have taken a polytechnical approach to design by engaging in a dialogue about nature vis-à-vis technology. We should not abandon this central concern by overemphasizing systems at the expense of tectonic issues, nor should our landscapes be designed to erase the fact of our presence as manipulators of the built environment. The educational aims of sustainable landscape design, which have become increasingly important to those who sponsor these projects as well as those who use them, provide opportunities for landscape architects to reframe the discussion about what constitutes "nature" given that these sites are being remade from the ground up. Hargreaves Associates' work is important to this conversation because it incorporates the functional aspects of sustainability into site features and experiential sequences, but challenges the conventional forms that many of these legislative mandates have taken. Nor does the firm treat its projects as the replication of a presumed former state to which the landscape must be returned. Though no one knows what unadulterated nature would look like, images of what it is presumed to be are ubiquitous, especially when it comes to parks. Hargreaves Associates' use of contrasting planting and maintenance strategies that reinforce the patently constructed topography is a means to resist such interpretations.

All landscapes are ecological because energy flows through them; they support human and animal habitat; and they can be measured according to various criteria, which would make them more or less sustainable depending on what criteria are used. A change in ethics gives rise to different landscapes, which is why we now conserve or make wetlands rather than fill them in (at least in theory), an ethic that arose out of new information about the ecological function of wetlands.[40] Yet can a particular landscape directly lead to a restructuring of beliefs? The relationship between design intent and reception will be taken up in more detail in the next chapter; however, as is clear in Guadalupe River Park, the treatment of the river as dynamic and fluctuating is apparent in the design itself, yet some will interpret the result as offering a unique experience of an urban river, while others will view it as a lost opportunity to restore a habitat. In other words, landscapes do not convey ethics, people do. For this reason, there can be no neutrality, or apolitically conceived definitions of function or sustainability. While many will admit to the multifaceted nature of sustainability (that it has ideological and political content, not just ecological and economic content), there are those who argue that sustainable landscapes are "in contrast to landscape as appealing mainly to the eye or aspiring cerebrally to be fine art. More succinctly, landscape architecture is about making fit places which fit."[41] Why does making a "fit place" have little or nothing to do with how it

appears, or how it might be intellectually challenging? For Hargreaves, the notion of fitting has as much to do with social and cultural uses as with ecological ones, as much to do with providing a range of activities as with creating a single understanding of fitness. Ultimately, Hargreaves believes that the only sustainable landscapes are ones that are well loved, because they will be the longest lasting.[42] While determining what is well loved is as elusive as defining "fitness," Hargreaves Associates' work suggests that a project will have a greater chance of success if it can appeal to a wide range of sensibilities and uses, and also challenge our sensibilities, however "cerebral" that notion may seem.

All landscapes are technological because they are manipulated. Landscapes are designed according to controls imposed from the outside (laws, site limitations, etc.) and controls used by designers (aesthetic, symbolic, and technical criteria) to form them in a particular way. Landscape processes—cleansing, directing, infiltrating, and growing—are engineered systems, though the proposed forms cannot be reduced to quantifying such systems. What constitutes a meaningful engagement with technology in the landscape changes as our understanding and depiction of the relationship between organic and mechanic processes changes. Landscape architecture is the practice that addresses this affiliation, and techniques—the methods we use to design, construct, and maintain our landscapes—are the means to achieve new formations of this relationship.

SYDNEY OLYMPIC PARK

T HE SYDNEY OLYMPIC PARK development was the largest remediation project of its kind in Australia, encompassing an area of 640 hectares, two-thirds of which is parkland. Originally comprising salt- and freshwater wetlands, rivers, and creeks, large areas were gradually filled beginning in the late nineteenth century. The site had many uses, including as a storage area for munitions, as an abattoir (1911–88), brickworks, and from the 1920s on, for various kinds of chemical manufacturing. It was estimated that, by the late 1980s, contaminated soils and waste existed on more than half of the site. Its transformation from toxic ground to diverse parklands and mixed development began about twenty-five years ago with Australia's Bicentennial in 1988. Over 90 hectares were transformed into a regional recreation area, half of which was devoted to protecting wetlands and the other half to covering a municipal dump with Bicentennial Park. When Sydney won the bid for the 2000 Olympics, the remediation efforts for the remainder of the area were fast-tracked. A master plan was in place and construction under way when Hargreaves was brought in to create a landscape concept for the area that comprised the Olympic Park public spaces.[43] Hargreaves Associates worked with a governmental agency, the Government Architect's Design Directorate, to replan 256 hectares of development and park, and worked on the detailed development of parts of the master plan.

There are three principal elements in Hargreaves Associates' design: Olympic Boulevard, a vast, paved area that is the primary spine of Olympic Park; the preservation of large trees, along with the addition of densely planted trees along the boulevard and the streets that run perpendicular to it; and interactive water features to mark the high point (Fig Grove) and low point (Northern Water Feature) of Olympic Boulevard. With Sydney's bid to conduct the first "green games," water conservation and reuse was a substantial part of the development of the site's infrastructure, buildings, and landscape. The site utilizes an integrated water cycle that collects, cleans, and treats all sewage and stormwater on site for use in irrigation, fountains, and anything not directly consumed by people. It includes separate water mains for reclaimed water and drinking water, and a treatment plant to purify sewage and stormwater. The primary water storage reservoir is the former brick quarry (with observation walkway designed by Peter Walker and Partners) and secondary storage is a series of freshwater wetlands, which includes the Northern Water Feature wetland designed by Hargreaves Associates.

The early study models indicate the importance of Olympic Boulevard as the central pedestrian spine of the project but also illustrate that water was a key element used to conceptually link the north and south ends of the site. The models, made with clay and paper, show the boulevard terminating at the creek to the north, which is where the Northern Water Feature sits, but also show a reconfigured creek (called Boundary Creek) at its southern terminus, a creek that drains into the constructed lake in Bicentennial Park (built in 1988 to cover the municipal dump). The water bodies are expressed as a circuit, one that links existing freshwater wetlands and streams, constructed water bodies, and mangroves. Though these would not have been physically connected by surface water (some are freshwater, some are saltwater; some are used for treatment, others are not), they are made to abut each other so that one could conceivably follow the circuit of water along its different functions and expressions. In the end, there were very few changes made to Boundary Creek and none to Bicentennial Park, since their water bodies, reconfigured in 1988, are not part of the integrated stormwater management and harvesting plan. Nevertheless, the bold line of Olympic Boulevard connects them.

FIGURE 73. Location map drawn by Keith VanDerSys and Agnes Ladjevardi.

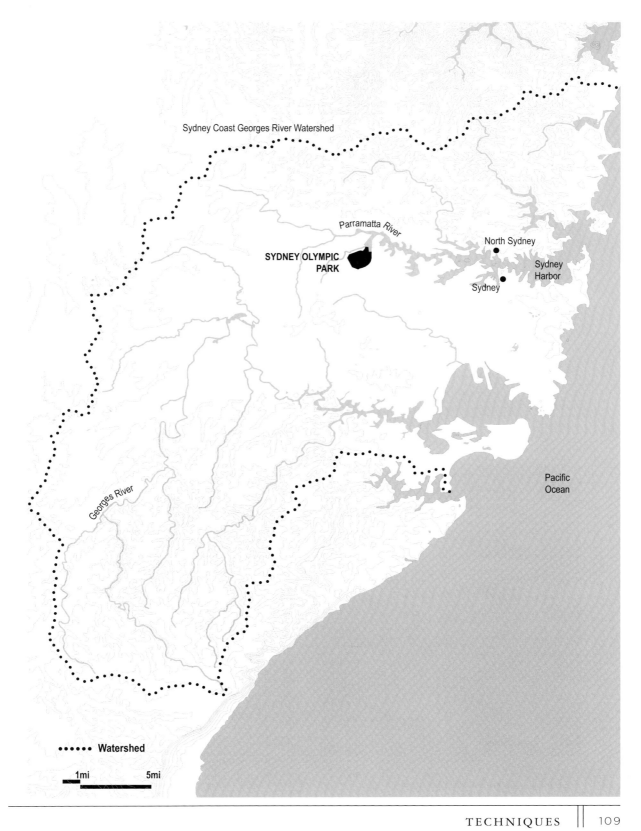

Sydney Coast Georges River Watershed

Parramatta River

SYDNEY OLYMPIC PARK

North Sydney

Sydney Harbor

Sydney

Georges River

Pacific Ocean

●●●●● Watershed

1mi   5mi

Parklands Plan of Management (2010)

3.10. Plan 4 – Parklands Remediated Lands

The Remediated Lands Plan identifies those areas where waste material has been compacted and stored underground and are subject to long term management obligations under the Remediated Land Management Plan 2009 and a Notice under the Contaminated Land Management Act 1997.

FIGURE 75. Hargreaves was hired after construction on the stadiums had already begun. The firm designed a large, patterned surface to give identity to the central space and unify the buildings. The Northern Water Feature can be seen at the top of the plan, and Fig Grove fountain in the center of the plan (in a very different configuration at the time of this plan; it is located where the square grove is shown). Even though Boundary Creek and Lake Belvedere (bottom of drawing) were not reconfigured for the 2000 games, this drawing shows them as primary components of the concept of east-west and north-south connections and shows the importance of water as a primary element in the planning.

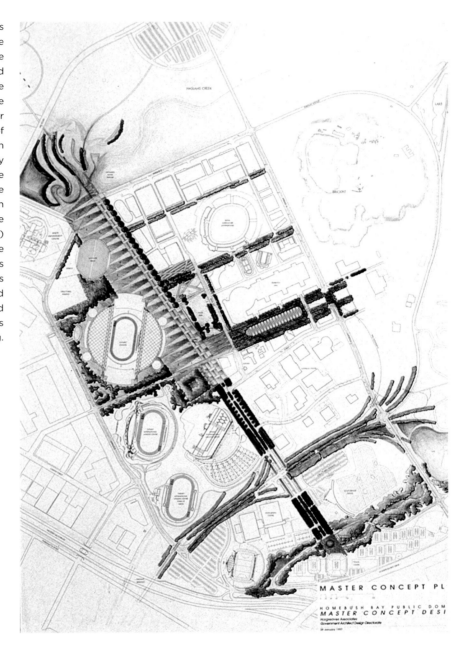

MASTER CONCEPT PL

HOMEBUSH BAY PUBLIC DOM
MASTER CONCEPT DESI

OPPOSITE

FIGURE 74. This drawing shows the extent of the parkland plan surrounding the Sydney Olympic venues. It was determined that the toxic soil should be buried beneath a layer of clay in large mounds that dot the site (shown in yellow), rather than moving it elsewhere. AUSIMAGE © Sinclair Knight Merz Pty Ltd.

FIGURE 76. Initial study models show the primary elements Hargreaves Associates used to tie the site together conceptually and geometrically. This model shows the plan similar to the original master plan that was in place before Hargreaves was hired, which had a primary street running north-south (Olympic Boulevard, shown as a red line).

BOTTOM

FIGURE 77. This model illustrates east-west connections that tie into Olympic Boulevard, a surface that surrounds half of the boulevard (central area shown in blue), and areas that are reconfigured on the ends of the boulevard (also blue). The cut at the south end shows an expanded Boundary Creek and visible connection to Lake Belvedere in Bicentennial Park.

FIGURES 78 AND 79. These models show expanded blue zones around Olympic Boulevard. This image (Figure 79) is closest to the final design: Boundary Creek and Lake Belvedere are untouched and there is an expanded zone around the northern half of Olympic Boulevard. In the final scheme, this zone contained the two water features while the majority of it is paved with a porous paving system to allows rain to infiltrate.

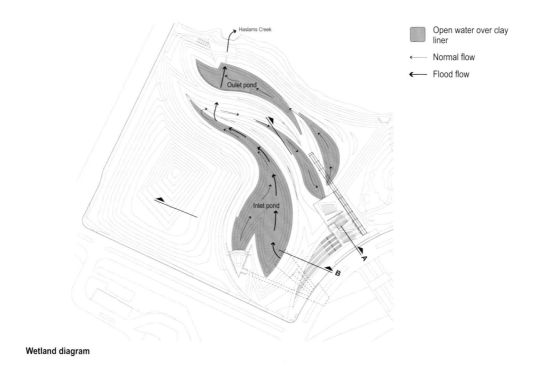

Open water over clay liner
← Normal flow
← Flood flow

Haslams Creek

Oulet pond

Inlet pond

A

B

Wetland diagram

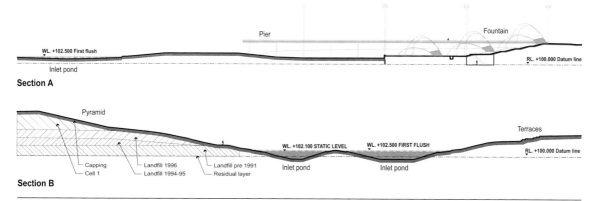

Pier

Fountain

WL. +102.500 First flush

RL. +100.000 Datum line

Inlet pond

Section A

Pyramid

Terraces

WL. +102.100 STATIC LEVEL   WL. +102.500 FIRST FLUSH

RL. +100.000 Datum line

Capping   Landfill 1996   Landfill pre 1991   Inlet pond   Inlet pond
Cell 1   Landfill 1994-95   Residual layer

Section B

FIGURE 80. Though the shape of the wetland was flexible, the cross-section and water levels must be carefully controlled in order for the wetland to have optimal function for plant survival and settlement of sediment. The plan drawing shows the water flow from the stormwater inlet to its outlet into Haslams Creek. Section A shows the proximity of the water fountain and pool to the wetland edge, and the pier that is the terminus of Olympic Boulevard. Section B shows the original landfill layers and key water levels in the inlet pond. Redrawn by Keith VanDerSys and Agnes Ladjevardi based on information provided by Hargreaves Associates.

FIGURE 81. The Northern Water Feature consists of two parts: the rectangular pool (seen on the right)—where jets of water sprayed from the fountain land—and the wetland itself (seen center and left). Though they appear connected, the pool is perched above the wetland (as can be seen in this image and the previous section drawing) and the two water systems remain separate; however, they are indirectly connected. This wetland, and others in the parkland, captures rainwater, which is sent for cleansing to one of the treatment plants. This recycled water is then used in the fountains, irrigation, and other site functions. The terminus of Olympic Boulevard is the elevated walkway that extends over the wetland. Image courtesy of John Gollings.

FIGURE 82. Fig Grove Fountain sits at the center point, also the high point, of Olympic Boulevard. Image courtesy of John Gollings.

FIGURE 83. The triangular cut of Fig Grove Fountain is mirrored in the pyramidal mound adjacent to the Northern Water Feature. Image courtesy of John Gollings.

FIGURE 89. The portion of the river for which the project was halted, and eventually left intact, can be seen in the background (left) of this image. In the foreground is the invert, designed by Sasaki Associates, which allows the water to bypass the intact riparian vegetation and where Hargreaves Associates had intended to locate the flood meadow. This photo was taken from West Santa Clara Street looking north. Photograph by Dvortygirl.

FIGURE 90. Further upstream material differences create a layered effect. The lower area is made with gabions, while the upper terraces are stone surfaces. The two zones are planted with different species and the lower zone is not irrigated. Photograph by the author.

FIGURE 91. An image of the northern areas of the park after grading was completed.

FIGURE 92. The grasses on the landforms soften their edges and the trees have matured. The landforms and shadows create a rhythmic effect when one looks across them. Image courtesy of Ken McCown.

BRIGHTWATER WASTE-WATER TREATMENT FACILITY

BRIGHTWATER WASTEWATER TREATMENT Facility and Northern Mitigation Area is a 114-acre site located in Snohomish County, Washington. The northern one-third of the site contained degraded wetlands, streams—some of which were buried in pipes—and partial forest cover, while the other two-thirds had been used as auto salvage yards with office buildings and warehouses. The design and construction has progressed in two phases based on the distinction between these two zones: the North 40 Mitigation (N40) area, which sits outside of the urban growth boundary, was treated as a salmon habitat restoration and reforestation effort and was part of the public mitigation; the Treatment Plant area within the urban growth boundary contains a secured zone—with all the treatment facilities—and 30 acres of publicly accessible landscape that detains and treats the on-site rainwater. The landscapes of these two zones contain new or reconstituted wetlands but are otherwise distinct in their formal and planting tactics. Both areas required engineering in order to improve the quality of soil, water, and vegetation for both habitat and stormwater functions.

The landforms in the N40 area are egg-shaped hills surrounded by the conserved and replanted forest; the hills are bilaterally symmetrical in plan and are planted with meadow grasses, while the forest is developed in a grid layout with each segment containing a specific quantity and mixture of species. In contrast, the majority of landforms fronting the Treatment Plant facilities are gently arcing and triangular or trapezoidal in profile. They are syncopated to provide views into the treatment facility, alternately exposing and concealing the buildings when viewed from the road. In the area of the Treatment Plant, vegetation is arrayed largely in correspondence with the landforms, wherein each side of a landform is planted with a different combination of plants. The top edges of the landforms are outlined with a single or double row of trees. The largest, southernmost landform on the site is a hybrid of the approaches taken in the N40 and Treatment Plant areas.

Hargreaves Associates' design transforms the site into a landscape that displays different landform and vegetation tactics as much as it constitutes a restoration effort. The approach does not emulate nature's appearance, or what we've come to understand as nature's appearance, but instead frames natural processes with contrasting and varied landscape elements. The highly engineered nature of the landscape will become less evident as vegetation fills in. Educational tours and placards will inform visitors of the landscape's various functions, but the contrasting forms and planting will help maintain its legibility as a constructed landscape.

FIGURE 93. Location map drawn by Keith VanDerSys and Agnes Ladjevardi.

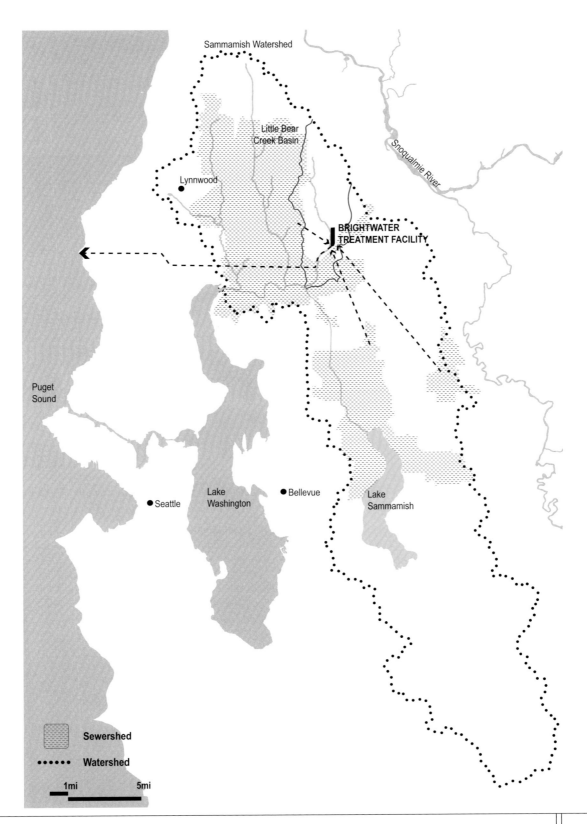

Sammamish Watershed

Little Bear
Creek Basin

Snoqualmie River

Lynnwood

BRIGHTWATER
TREATMENT FACILITY

Puget
Sound

Seattle

Lake
Washington

Bellevue

Lake
Sammamish

Sewershed

Watershed

1mi   5mi

Figure labels on map (from top-left area): UNNAMED CREEK OVERLOOK; FIELD HOUSE & GARDEN; MEADOW HILLS; MITIGATION FORESTED WETLAND; ROUTE 522; UPLAND FOREST; UPPER UNNAMED CREEK; UPPER POND; BOARDWALK OVERLOOK; LOWER UNNAMED CREEK; MITIGATION WETLAND; BOARDWALK; LOWER POND; EDUCATION AND COMMUNITY CENTER; NORTH WETSCAPE; ROUTE 4; POND OVERLOOK; SOUTH WETSCAPE; BOARDWALK; LITTLE BEAR CREEK; STORMWATER PONDS; MITIGATION WETLAND; HOWELL CREEK

Brightwater
TREATMENT SYSTEM

KING COUNTY — Department of Natural Resources and Parks, Wastewater Treatment Division   CH2MHILL   MITHUN   HARGREAVES ASSOCIATES

FIGURE 94. The forested area to the north (N40) did not have contamination and already contained some streams and vegetative cover. The design includes a trail system, observation bridges for viewing wetlands and salmon-spawning pools, and a salmon-rearing pond. There were over twenty-two thousand plants planted just on this portion of the site; recycling of felled trees for use in the stream and pond reconstruction; almost fourteen hundred feet of stream restored, surfaced from underground pipes; and four acres of emergent and forested wetland habitat created, as well as two-thirds of an acre of pond habitat that connects two open wetland systems. The southern two-thirds of the site was largely composed of impervious surface and some limited subsurface contamination from former uses. The area to the west of the building facilities has various arcing landforms strung along a line of constructed wetlands for stormwater treatment. (Note: Figures 94 and 95 are oriented with north pointing left.)

OPPOSITE

FIGURE 95. This diagram shows how the stormwater flows through the landscape. This stormwater collection system is entirely independent from the functions of the Treatment Plant and no water from within the plant is treated in the landscape (except for groundwater feeds from under drains beneath the treatment tanks, which do not include sewage water). The habitat restoration area is also separate from the stormwater collection ponds in the Treatment Plant area, their waters only joining together at the adjacent Little Bear Creek. Redrawn by Keith VanDerSys based on information provided by Hargreaves Associates and Michael Popiwny from King County, Washington.

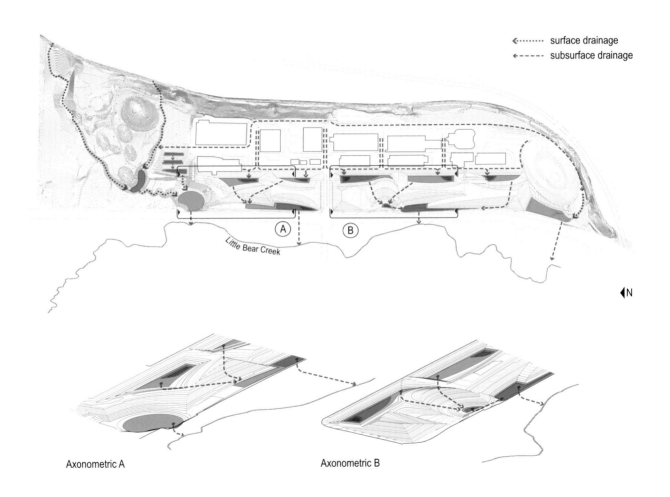

surface drainage
subsurface drainage

Little Bear Creek

Ⓐ   Ⓑ

◀N

Axonometric A

Axonometric B

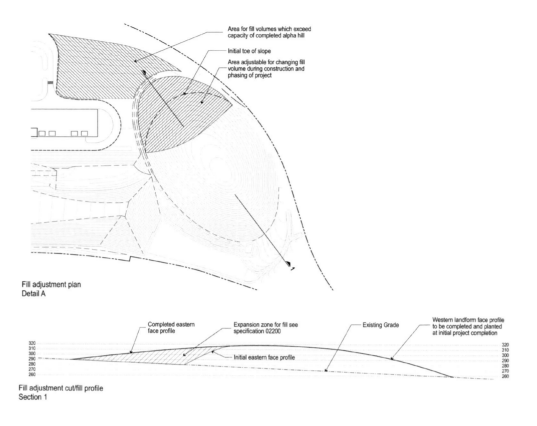

Area for fill volumes which exceed
capacity of completed alpha hill

Initial toe of slope

Area adjustable for changing fill
volume during construction and
phasing of project

Fill adjustment plan
Detail A

Completed eastern
face profile

Expansion zone for fill see
specification 02200

Existing Grade

Western landform face profile
to be completed and planted
at initial project completion

320
310
300
290
280
270
260

Initial eastern face profile

320
310
300
290
280
270
260

Fill adjustment cut/fill profile
Section 1

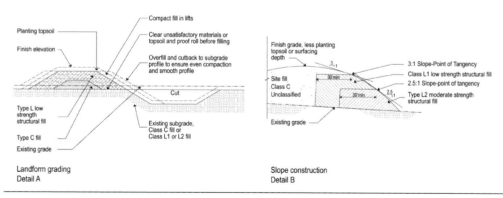

Planting topsoil

Finish elevation

Compact fill in lifts

Clear unsatisfactory materials or
topsoil and proof roll before filling

Overfill and cutback to subgrade
profile to ensure even compaction
and smooth profile

Cut

Type L low
strength
structural fill

Type C fill

Existing grade

Existing subgrade,
Class C fill or
Class L1 or L2 fill

Landform grading
Detail A

Finish grade, less planting
topsoil or surfacing
depth

3:1

Site fill
Class C
Unclassified

30'min

30'min

2.5:1

Existing grade

3:1 Slope-Point of Tangency

Class L1 low strength structural fill

2.5:1 Slope-point of tangency

Type L2 moderate strength
structural fill

Slope construction
Detail B

FIGURE 96. With the engineers, Hargreaves Associates designed the topography to account for unknown volumes of fill material (top drawing). The sections (bottom) show the typical details required for slope stabilization. Redrawn by Keith VanDerSys and Agnes Ladjevardi based on information provided by Hargreaves Associates.

FIGURE 97. The large landforms in the northern part of the site will be mowed annually to maintain their open, meadow character in contrast to the forested areas that encircle them.

FIGURE 98. As with any formerly industrial land, the sites have been stripped of their ability to support a diversity of habitat. In order to restore this ability, the landscape must be engineered. For example, the construction of the waterways at Brightwater involves a variety of soil mixtures to support a diverse range of environments including fish-rearing ponds, emergent wetlands, wet meadows, and upland meadows. Each habitat requires the appropriate soil profile to achieve the desired absorption for particular plant species. For large areas depleted of topsoil in the North 40 area, soil making was required to be simple and inexpensive, and was achieved by recycling materials found on site—sifting and clearing compost and landscape debris—from a previous landscape contracting business. This image shows cardboard being laid under the mulch to help with moisture retention and act as weed retardant. It will decompose along with the mulch surface, providing a growing medium for vegetation.

FIGURE 99. The terraced slopes in part of the mitigated wetland area in N40 are stabilized with geotextiles to prevent erosion.

FIGURE 100. The same view after three years of growth. Photograph by the author.

FIGURE 101. A view of the pond overlook on the southwest portion of the Treatment Plant area after initial planting.

FIGURE 102. A view of one of the stormwater ponds in the Treatment Plant area. The different water levels can be seen in the gradient of vegetation. One of the angular mounds can be seen in the center-right of the image, and the largest mound on the site can be seen in the background beyond the building facilities. Photograph by the author.

nothing about the "native" topography would suggest the type of grading in the firm's work. And while this "amplified" ground might appear static to some, it has the opposite effect experientially because of the variably scaled spaces it results in. Indeed, Hargreaves has said that what he finds most misunderstood about the firm's work is when it is criticized for being formulaic because it appears to be "all the same."[12] In other words, the work has a recognizable style, which for some equates to being superficial or acontextual; however, style is not merely an unnecessary by-product attached to something else that is allegedly more essential.[13] Such a reading belies the substantial sectional variation found in the work, and overlooks the complex relationship between a landscape's forms and materials. To be clear, the term "form" refers to the organizing structures of the landscape, which should be understood in multiple and simultaneously occurring ways. "Form" refers to the sculpting of the ground itself—the shape and directionality of topography—but it also refers to the geometries that set up overall site organization, which are often drawn from patterns or structures that lie beyond the site proper, such as street grids and bridges. These geometries—or regulating lines—are not necessarily continually marked on the ground, but they guide the overall formation of the projects, and are used to demarcate spatial orientation and material change. These two types of formation cor-

FIGURE 103. The landforms in front of the University of Cincinnati's DAAP building (designed by Peter Eisenman) look as if they have been displaced by the thrust of the building. Hargreaves saved the existing trees yet still managed to work around them with a dynamic form. Image courtesy of John Gollings.

FIGURE 104. The conical landform (foreground) "collides" with a pyramidal landform at the University of Cincinnati's Commons. Image courtesy of John Gollings.

respond at some times (topography follows the regulating lines), and diverge at others times (topographic form is not drawn from the regulating lines). In any event, form is not simply the shape of a "thing"; form is relational. It is a mechanism to directly (experientially) connect the scale of the body to the surrounding environment. Form can simultaneously point beyond the site by drawing one's attention outward and provide moments of spatial or visual concentration within. In other words, form is used to construct reciprocity between extensive and intensive environments: near and far, open and closed, expansive and sheltered; surroundings and site, connectivity and concentration. Hargreaves Associates' work is characterized by striving to engage both scales simultaneously.

Form is often considered determinate and static, whereas processes are seen as animate and contingent. Given this distinction, it would be easy to say that Hargreaves Associates' early work is more dynamic than its later work because the cycles of time (entropy, material fluctuation) are readily visible in projects like Candlestick Point Park and Guadalupe River Park. As noted in the preface, the firm's work has been described, both by Hargreaves and others, as representing a shift from a subjective engagement with landscape processes to a more collective engagement via program.[14] While it is clear that the different programs (the activities and functions a park must support) and project locations have effected changes in the character of the work, dynamic qualities are still constructed in the firm's projects in intentional ways. Rather than think of form as constant and material as dynamic, we need to remember that the perception of form is dynamic because of movement through, and change in, the landscape.[15] Though forms themselves do not change, the effects they create involve movement in other ways based on how circulation routes are configured in relation to them, the ever-changing shadows they produce, the unscripted activities they instigate, and how temporal qualities such as color and light alter our understanding of form. It is through formal "controls" that change can be so clearly registered in the landscape. Thus, in order to avoid the dichotomy between the "fixed" (form) and "fluid" (material and movement) aspects of landscape, what follows are examples in Hargreaves Associates' work that exemplify different rates of change—categorized as cycles and rhythms—and how the dynamic interplay among form, material, and movement is orchestrated in the work in order to instigate moments of awareness in the landscape.

CYCLES

SOCIAL EVENTS—concerts, festivals, markets—have, as Hargreaves says, their own "metes and bounds,"[16] cycles that mark our lives and become embedded in the practices of a place. The landscape must be designed to support these events; yet it can also be designed to coexist and accentuate the rhythms and cycles embedded in the materiality of landscape itself. Hargreaves's distinction between operation (intentional and made) and process (unmade—it is "what happens") is useful here.[17] Designers deal with the former but can do so in ways that frame, support, or guide the latter. For example, Louisville Waterfront Park might appear to be less in flux than a project like Candlestick Point Park, yet it undergoes more types of transformation (flooding, frequent large crowds, color change). This understanding is available only to frequent users rather than to one-time visitors, which is why Candlestick Point Park might result in a more consistent set of experiences on multiple visits. At Louisville Waterfront Park, the lawn slopes dramatically toward the river, allowing it to become inundated by water during heavy rains. This tactic combines an aesthetic based on stasis, order, and control (lawn) with one based on movement, disturbance, and messiness (flood). The cyclical flooding is seasonal, happening most often in the spring, but it does not occur at regular intervals, as do the more predictable seasonal changes of vegetation. This flooding results in a temporary interruption in use and perceived edges, as what appear to be cleanly delineated zones and a well-defined path system are partially effaced. When the lawn is

FIGURES 105 AND 106. During heavy rains, the rising Ohio River deposits large logs and debris onto the lawn at Louisville Waterfront Park. The benches that sit on the end of the lawn are partially submerged. Images courtesy of Susan P. Case.

flooded various paths dead-end into water, an occurrence that happens at least six times per year.[18] The difference between what appears to be a conventional park feature—a large lawn with paved circulation tracing its edges—and its actuality is incongruous.

Of course Hargreaves Associates is not the only firm to employ an approach that invites fluctuation. Other well-known, contemporaneous examples include Herbert Bayer's Mill Creek Canyon Earthworks (1982), comprising pronounced forms, such as earthen rings and conical mounds, which become filled with water, or appear to rise above it, as the creek running through the site swells.[19] Another is Michael Van Valkenburgh Associates' Mill Race Park (1989–93), which is the same size as Louisville Waterfront Park. It sits within a flood-plain where it gets frequently inundated; however, as with Bayer's project, the way that topography and other structures are employed within the park appear more as independent elements and figures scattered throughout a basin, rather than an entire ground that is composed and orientated toward the surrounding features that constitute the site (the geometries of adjacent roads and bridges, as well as the river itself). For example, the edge of the lawn at Louisville Waterfront Park sits five feet above normal pool level and so it does not become inundated with every rain. However, the slope of the lawn and its open edge is a gesture that invites the "externality" of the river into the site, even when the site is dry. The river is immediately present as soon as one crosses the threshold from the street or sidewalk into the park.

ages people to veer off the paths and scale the topography. On multiple days I spent at Louisville Waterfront Park and the Clinton Presidential Center, people were standing atop the highest hills, kids running and rolling down them, and a family cardboard sledding. In other words, form isn't simply inspired by motion (as in the river flow at Louisville, Guadalupe River Park, and the University of Cincinnati), it also invokes motion, resulting in a highly varied and tactile experience of the landscape.

From aerial and plan views of Louisville Waterfront Park, it is difficult to see just how distinct the linear park area is in contrast to the more planar spaces of the adjacent great lawn, outlook terrace, water feature, and plaza and wharf, all of which are open to the street. The geometry of these areas is drawn from the regulating lines that were derived from the adjacent street grid and the bridges that cross the Ohio River. To heighten differences between the large gathering spaces of the plaza, wharf, and lawn, the designers inserted a long, stepped fountain and a shaded terrace between them. The "fill" of the terrace and the "cut" of the fountain, with its large sprays of water directed toward the river, are perched between the wharf area and the lawn, which are the two areas that regularly flood. The fountain is a zone that is always animated (fountain sprays, the sound of rushing water that drowns out the noise of a nearby freeway, people playing in it, etc.). A second large cut—an inlet—on the opposite side of the lawn is used for boat docking and must be kept clear of debris. A third cut, a smaller inlet, exists within the linear park area and was thought to be self-purging of debris; how-

ever, it has evolved into a wetland full of cattails and birds. These recurring cuts and the paths that trace their edges offer distinct experiences. The paths ascend and descend through these various zones rather than trace a linear progression from the city toward the river, or from more controlled to more wild. No two areas of the park are the same, yet the repetition of both the topographic forms and the regulating lines is readily apparent, thereby showcasing and alternating different relationships between formal structures and material cycles in close succession.

The Clinton Presidential Center site is simpler, being one-third the size of Louisville Waterfront Park, but it is also characterized by a repetitive organization that is used to create distinct landscape zones. On the northwest quadrant of the site, there are three paths that run roughly east-west: the upper edge of the plateau (which is called President Clinton Avenue and is on axis with the building entrance), the lower walk by the wetland, and a diagonal walk that connects them. The north-south paths that lead from the plateau down to the wetland are steps that intersect all three east-west paths. These north-south paths slope at the same rate, yet the spaces between the paths are formed by a remarkable faceted topography that alternates between depressions, thereby opening up vistas in one direction, and inclines, which "enclose" the paths. As at Louisville, this approach is not an immersive, all-encompassing effect where the park is a place of remove, but rather a topography that is structured as an intermediary between concentrated effects of activity, shadow, enclosure, and the extensive relationships set up by the lines of paths and topo-

FIGURE 110. At Louisville Waterfront Park, debris can be seen collecting in the smaller of the two inlets soon after construction (facing east). The level pathway continues along the water's edge and a second path zigzags up to the Linear Park picnic areas.

FIGURE 111. On the opposite side of the inlet and facing west, the inlet has filled in with sediment over time. This photo was taken in May 2004. Image courtesy of Matthew Jolley.

FIGURE 112. The same inlet is seen here in September 2011 (also facing west). It has become a wetland filled with numerous species of plants. Photograph by the author.

FIGURE 113. The pathway that snakes behind the wetland, which used to have views open to the inlet and river (on the right) as seen in Figures 110 and 111, is now an enclosed and intimate path. Photograph by the author.

graphic high points. The biggest disappointment at the Clinton Presidential Center site was that the second phase (the recently completed wetland) was not built according to Hargreaves Associates' design. Hargreaves's design extended the long lines of the north-south paths farther north to form alternating zones of lawn and wetland areas. These paths were intended to bridge to a small bar of land that demarcates the wetland area from the Arkansas River, thereby providing access to the river's edge. Importantly, from the ridge (President Clinton Avenue) these lines would lead the eye to the river, which is largely camouflaged by vegetation. In other words, the landscape was equally oriented toward the river and the building. Unfortunately, what was built is a somewhat clichéd, themed version of wetland—themed because it is internally focused (its geometry is a loose, curvilinear meander, also known as "naturalistic"). Also, its detailing is "rustic" (what you might find in a remote state park) with open-shed structures scattered about its walkways. It is a formal and material response that does not consider anything else around it, especially the relationships set up by Hargreaves Associates and Polshek Partnership, the designers of the building.

Of course, Hargreaves Associates' projects never "fit" (look like) their surroundings either, but they are nevertheless oriented to their surroundings. They use innovative form to create unique places (they are legible at the local scale) that simultaneously point beyond the site (through regulating lines and the orientation of the topography) and invite chance and change into the site (through regulating lines that form cuts and create alternations between static and dynamic materials). The

low-lying area at the Clinton Presidential Center— both in Hargreaves Associates' design and the one that was actually built—is composed of a wetland. Visitors to both the Hargreaves' designed landscape and the built one would experience a wetland, and see many of the same birds and plants. Whether or not this experience could lead to a reorienting of values is unknown; certainly the two versions of wetland could contain the same placards with information as to the wetland's environmental functions, such as habitat creation and water decontamination. However, in Hargreaves Associates' design, the geometry of the constructed wetland is part of the same organization that comprises the building, the parking, and the pillowed topography; the wetland is not presented as "other." The fact that all aspects of the landscape are part of the same system but reordered to show varying degrees of structure in relation to process would be perceptually clear to those who would have experienced this landscape. Both Hargreaves Associates' design and the wetland that was built have a "style," but style is clearly the result of different attitudes toward relationships (site-surrounding, constructed-natural environments, form-material, operation-process). To not concern ourselves with so-called decorative or stylistic concerns is to not concern ourselves with the efficacy of design for setting up these relationships at perceptible scales.

CONCLUSION

THE DOUBLE MEANING OF EFFECT—appearance and influence, perception and cognition—forms the basis of divergent interpretations about a landscape's ability to stimulate interest, and whether or not that interest can be transformed into specific knowledge or understanding. It goes without saying that knowledge informs perception, and different ethical and cultural frameworks color our aesthetic responses; therefore, it is important to avoid conflating legibility, communication, interpretation, and knowledge. To put it most succinctly, Luhmann asserts that the relationship between perception and communication in art is "irritating and defies normality—*and just this is communicated.*"[22] However, this gap between a designer's intent and a user's perception of the resultant design should not be misconstrued to say that the meaning invested by the designer does not matter. This conflation is irrelevant. Designs are formed as they are because of the ambitions of the designer with respect to broader cultural issues (conversations on the nature of nature, public space, place), in response to specific requests or demands (by client, users, legislation), via a designer's own aesthetic predilections and values. The intentions of the designer are what give a work its particular form and perceptible attributes. Designers make environments, atmospheres, and effects for the purpose of creating experiences, guiding awareness, and promoting activities, though they can never delimit what these are (in other words, the search for meaning is constrained by the work without being determined in its results). This purpose allows for uncoupling specific emotive or didactic effects from the general ability of a work to appeal to the senses or to make relationships that direct our attention.

The most interesting of Hargreaves Associates' projects challenge conventional forms of landscape design. This has been done in different ways as the practice has evolved. For example, the follies and object-like landforms at Byxbee Park contribute to its unusual qualities; so too does its surface, which comprises unirrigated and infrequently maintained grasses. The same is true for allowing material fluctuation to be a major component of the design, such as Crissy Field's marsh, or Guadalupe River Park, which results in landscapes that undergo frequent modification. These designs are quite jarring in terms of our expectations because they question the image of verdant nature to which we have become accustomed, images that still dominate popular conceptions of landscape. So what about instances where Hargreaves Associates' work is normalized by the ubiquitous presence of lawn, the most static and familiar material blanketing our landscape? As is evident in projects such as Louisville Waterfront Park, the Clinton Presidential Center, and the University of Cincinnati, the conspicuous manipulation of topography generates dynamism in the work and provides the basis for other cycles to transform it—shadows, color, water, and public events. Though lawn covers large areas, there is no unified treatment of the landscape. Because of this fact, the firm's projects express and index different "natures": the analogical (forms inspired by the structure of natural formations), the wild (uncontrolled material fluctuation), the taxonomic (planting). These distinct approaches are placed adjacent to each other, thereby on equal ground, in order to contribute to an awareness of the landscape as a multiplicity of environments, which in turn can invoke multiple readings and uses.

To uncouple the relationship between the perceptible attributes of a work and its ethical efficacy is not at all to propose that we only concern ourselves with sensations and atmospheres without recourse to their significance.[23] But it is to say that the relationship between the two definitions of "effect" is indirect and unstable; rather, a work initiates a dynamic interplay between design intention and user perception, appearance and resonance, form and experience. Interviews with two key individuals within the organizations that manage and maintain Louisville Waterfront Park and the Clinton Presidential Center make clear that the notion of frameworks as being opposed to form and experience has little relevance. They see their respective projects as having transformed the larger area by attracting residents, business, and visitors (landscape as effective planning tool), while simultaneously providing people with space for activities they did not previously have access to (making places people want to go), and they understand the relationships that are set up by the design (directing our attention). And, remarkably, they described their projects, respectively, as "open-ended" and "continually evolving," then commented that what makes them so is it that they are always unfolding in surprising ways based on the people who make these places their own.[24]

LOUISVILLE WATERFRONT PARK

THE LOUISVILLE WATERFRONT DEVELOPment Corporation, formed in 1986, hired Hargreaves Associates to begin the master plan in 1990. The master plan encompasses 120 acres along the Ohio River in downtown Louisville. The park, covering 85 of these acres, was built in three phases over a fifteen-year period. Though the park is spatially diverse, accommodating both small pockets of activity and flat, open expanses for large events, Hargreaves Associates used repeating geometries and forms to provide a well-defined, legible organization to the whole.

The geometries, drawn from the street grid and from the bridges spanning the Ohio River, provided the basis for overlapping, regulating lines that order the primary circulation and large event spaces in the park. The modified topography ranges from relatively flat, paved terraces to large evenly sloped lawns, to sharply cut and steeply graded slopes. In the area that comprises the wharf, overlook terrace, and lawn, the fissures between these various planes provide sectional changes for steps and seating, or splay apart to let water into the site. A nine-hundred-foot-long fountain provides the most dramatic example of this phenomenon; it appears as a gap, pulling the river visually into the site, creating an immense playground of water. The form of the fountain is inspired by the Falls of the Ohio, where the river descends naturally through a series of limestone shelves. The fountain's segments step from the street down to the riverfront. Within each stepped zone a diagonal shelf, whose geometry registers the angle of the adjacent bridge, creates small waterfalls. This controlled display of water contrasts with the other cuts in the site, which are inlets that collect debris from the river.

In the "linear park" portion of the project a series of large wedge-shaped forms, which arc and slope toward the river, provide the overall organization for vehicular and pedestrian circulation; smaller, sinuous forms that sit within the larger ones provide more intimate spaces for other activities such as picnic areas and playgrounds. A continuous riverside path winds its way along the edge of this topography. When one travels along this path, the landforms create a rhythm alternating between steep embankments, with high points above eye level, and elongated views into lawn expanses. A series of paths splinter off this primary path to circle the smaller landforms.

The planting largely corresponds to the two overall topographic approaches. In the rectangular and triangular planes of the entry areas, plaza, and overlook, Hargreaves Associates employs allées and groves—lines and grids—to provide spatial definition. In the linear park areas, the planting reinforces the shapes of the topography. The steep sides of the large wedge-shaped landforms are oriented to River Road, and many are densely planted with evergreen trees and ground cover to provide a visual and acoustic buffer. On the more gradual slopes, which open up views toward the river, "drifts" of canopy trees are scattered across both the lawn and the smaller, sinuous landforms. The dark, dense planting contrasts with the canopy trees, especially in the autumn when the canopy turns brilliant red and golden hues. Gridded apple trees tucked in the flat areas on the south side of these large landforms surround the parking lots; they are visible from River Road, providing bursts of color and order against the height and mass of the evergreen trees.

TOP

FIGURE 120. On a hot July day, the fountain is busiest in the shade of the freeway. The walls that contain the water are based on one grid (the street) and the diagonal walls within the fountain that create the waterfall are based on the rotated grid (the bridge). Photograph by the author.

BOTTOM

FIGURE 121. The dramatic slope of the lawn underneath the freeway is evident in this photograph. Image courtesy of Matthew Jolley.

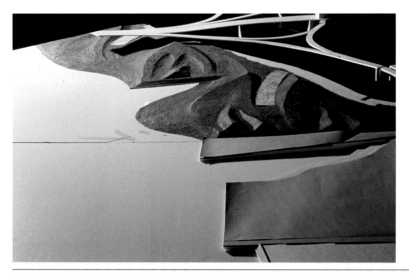

FIGURE 122. In the Linear Park area of the project, small landforms (the twin shapes that sit on top of the larger slopes) can be clearly seen in the model (looking east; north is to the left) and the next image (where north is up). The experience of the space can be seen in Figure 124.

FIGURE 123. A grading plan of the layering of topography in the Linear Park portion of the park is shown here. The inlet that has since evolved into a wetland can be seen at the top right of the plan and in Figures 110–113. Redrawn by Keith VanDerSys and Agnes Ladjevardi based on information provided by Hargreaves Associates.

FIGURE 124. This view, facing west, is of the shady area between two of the small landforms. The small ridges create an intimate zone but, because the larger form with which they merge is sloping, they simultaneously open up to views of the areas beyond. The lawn and overlook terrace are visible on the horizon. Image courtesy of Waterfront Development Corporation.

FIGURE 125. This photo is taken from atop one of the wedge-shaped figures that has long, arcing, low retaining walls inserted into its gradually sloping face. Photograph by the author.

FIGURE 126. The line of demarcation between maintained lawn and frequently flooded zone can be seen here. The upper pathway roughly demarcates the ten-year flood line in this part of the park; the lower path sits just above the normal high-water level. The areas that are brown become full of vegetation in the summer months and are cut back for winter. Image courtesy of Eugenio Roig.

UNIVERSITY OF CINCINNATI

Hargreaves Associates was hired in 1989 to develop a master plan for the University of Cincinnati after the university projected that it needed one million square feet of new building space. The firm's work comprised three primary master plan documents (in 1991, 1995, 2000), and in conjunction with the planning work, the firm designed the majority of the landscape projects associated with new and renovated buildings. Over the course of almost fifteen years, it built thirteen projects. These projects are small, most only a few acres in size, and quite distinct, but they aggregate to provide the "connective tissue" outlined in the master plan.

In the late 1800s, this campus began as a single, linear building situated on a ridge, with expansive views of the surrounding forests and ravine, giving a sense of place to this "university on a hill." A thoughtful relationship between building and landscape continued to define the University of Cincinnati's campus development until the postwar era, when it was granted land to expand, and auto-dominated design became the norm. The result was that, by the late 1980s, the campus had grown haphazardly, with no landscape planning to guide building location and configuration. Students would simply drive from class to class within the same area that defines the campus today. The challenge was to transform the campus from a commuter population into an on-campus living environment via a strong landscape framework so that the campus would not continue filling its core with isolated buildings and leftover, unformed exterior space. The difficulty was not simply to find room for new buildings, but to unite them in ways that, by necessity and choice, moved beyond the

FIGURE 132. This view is of Main Street, looking west, between the recreation center and retail space. Image courtesy of John Gollings.

FIGURE 133. This model shows Sigma Sigma Commons, the area adjoining Campus Green (the braided path can be seen in the top left quadrant of the image). A significant drop in elevation occurs here, which Hargreaves further accentuated by building up the topography into triangular and trapezoidal forms around the pathways. This creates a dramatic sense of enclosure and elevation change as one crosses the campus.

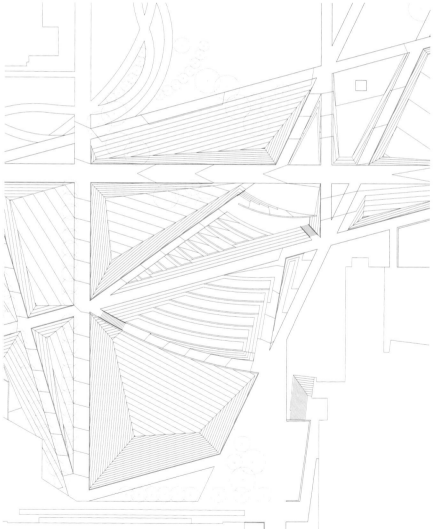

FIGURE 134. This grading plan shows the same area as the model. The intersecting paths and steep grade between them create a dynamic ground plane. Redrawn by Keith VanDerSys based on information provided by Hargreaves Associates.

FIGURE 135. This view is looking west in the area where the landform is terraced with massive stone steps. There is a path in the step above where the person is sitting, behind which the terraces become wider and grass-topped. Image courtesy of John Gollings.

FIGURE 136. This view of Sigma Sigma Commons is looking east. The terraced, grassed steps can be seen from this vantage. The steep embankments turn brilliant red in the fall. Image courtesy of Yan Da.

FIGURE 137. The northern part of the west campus had been leveled for a parking lot. Campus Green, part of which is shown in this grading plan, was inspired by the site's geologic history, designed to reintroduce a sense of movement and water flow based on the former ravine that ran through here. Hargreaves Associates created an interwoven series of paths, with serpentine landforms, to create a shifting horizon and enclose the space. The planting reinforces the curved shapes of the ground. On the right side of the image are triangular wedges that are shaded, gravel terraces. Redrawn by Keith VanDerSys based on information provided by Hargreaves Associates.

FIGURE 138. Inspired by the former ravine, Hargreaves created "waterfalls" along the braided path, made with stepped limestone. These areas can be approached from above or below. Image courtesy of John Gollings.

FIGURE 139. At the end of the braided path is a large, conical mound. It marks the northern edge of this portion of the campus and provides an iconic figure that can be seen along the large boulevard that sits north of it. In the fall, its surface, planted with winter creeper, turns brilliant red and is at its most prominent. As the trees of the braid turn their colors, the foreground and background merge into a red-hued environment. Image courtesy of Rich Whitehead.

BELOW

FIGURE 140. As one ascends the mound, views of the campus open up. Image courtesy of Addison Godel.

WILLIAM J. CLINTON PRESIDENTIAL CENTER PARK

T HE WILLIAM J. CLINTON PRESIDENTIAL Center is situated within thirty acres of parkland along the Arkansas River in Little Rock, Arkansas. The site had been previously used for light industrial purposes and contained abandoned warehouses and railroad tracks. A forty-five-foot bluff prohibited direct access to the river.

The site is organized by two grids that accommodate vehicular and pedestrian circulation, while they also subdivide the landscape according to different topographic and planting strategies. Polshek Partnership, the architectural firm for the building, responded to this organization by aligning the two building volumes with the different grids. The primary axis that runs through the middle of the site is essentially a ridge line: south of the line is a plateau made of planes of lawn, parking, and terraces; north of the line is lawn that adjoins both the extant riparian edge (east side of the building) and a lawn-covered faceted topography that provides a transition and access from the ridge down to the wetland (west side of the building). The tree planting also corresponds to the ridge line: the southern half of

FIGURE 141. The sculpted forms at the Clinton Presidential Center appear as folds or thrusts. The steep sides of the landforms were originally intended to be planted with groundcover, further accentuating the focus toward the river. The central east-west spine connects to an old railroad bridge (seen in the foreground) that was recently refurbished (not shown) to provide pedestrian access to North Little Rock. Image courtesy of Tim Hursley.

the site is planted in rows, grids, and groves, whereas the north side is planted with loosely spaced drifts of trees. Only the straight, stepped paths leading directly to the wetland break this structure and are lined with rows of trees. When walking along the ridge on the west side of the building, one sees flat ground to one side and alternating inclines and depressions to the other. The north-south stepped paths provide experiences of similar oscillating rhythms, due to the rise and fall of the adjacent topography. The design intent for the east side of the building was to have lawn with ordered trees on one side of the primary path, and alternating tall grass mixtures on the other side.

The firm designed the topography with clay and then translated it to drawings. Designers molded the clay to create unusual figures that draw the eye and entice people into the landscape, then scanned the model and, using the scanned image as a base, drew the grading plan over it. Though the landforms were not inspired by the geology of the area, the project recalls the larger region within which it is situated at the intersection of the Ouachita Mountains and the Mississippi alluvial plain. The town of Little Rock sits on a large outcropping, where the foothills of the Ouachitas form a plateau above the floodplain of the Arkansas River. The mountains are "fold mountains," resulting from seismic upheavals that buckled the rock, resulting in tilted formations. These particular mountains are unique because their ridges are oriented east-west, which means their slopes face south and north. In many ways, the structure of the topography evokes a similar force, appearing to thrust upward or fold.

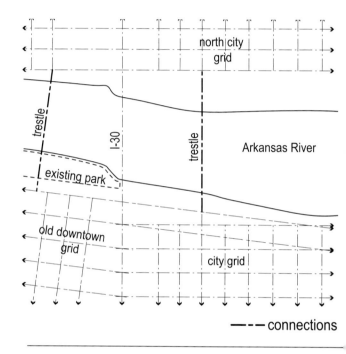

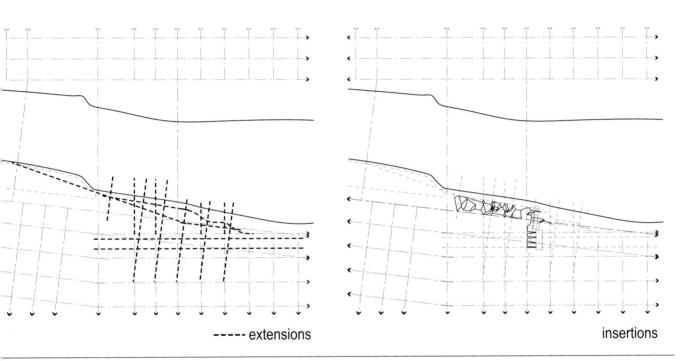

----- extensions

insertions

FIGURE 142. The "connections" show the layout of Little Rock and North Little Rock situated on the banks of the Arkansas River. Hargreaves Associates overlaid the old downtown grid of Little Rock across the newer grid, which shares the same geometry as that of North Little Rock. The overlapped grids—"Extensions"—create the overall framework for both landscape and building. "Insertions" are individual landforms that remain within the squares of the grid but break free from their geometry. Redrawn by Keith VanDerSys based on information provided by Hargreaves Associates..

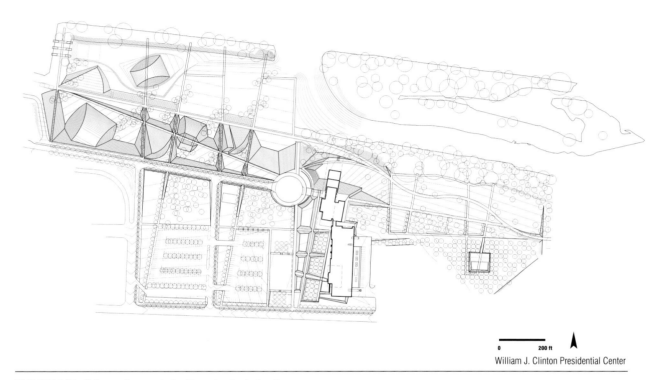

0   200 ft

William J. Clinton Presidential Center

FIGURE 143. This grading and planting plan includes the
future chapel (the square in the bottom right) surrounded by
a grove, and what was to be the future walkway extensions
over the wetland. The northwest part of this plan was not
built according to Hargreaves's design.

PLANTING

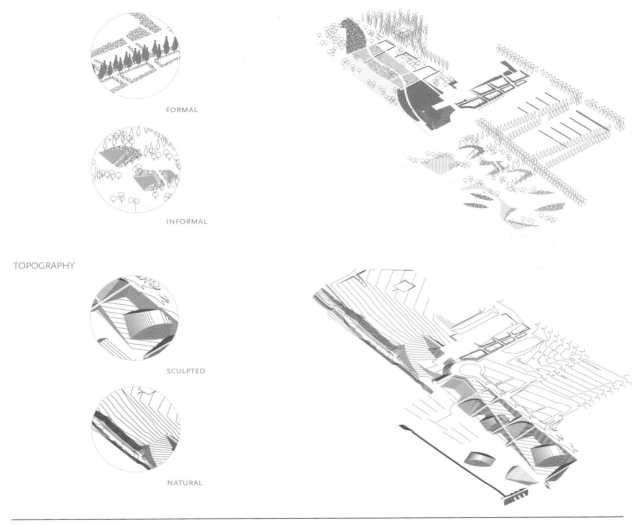

FORMAL

INFORMAL

TOPOGRAPHY

SCULPTED

NATURAL

FIGURE 144. The relationship between topography and vegetation as originally intended can be seen in these diagrams.

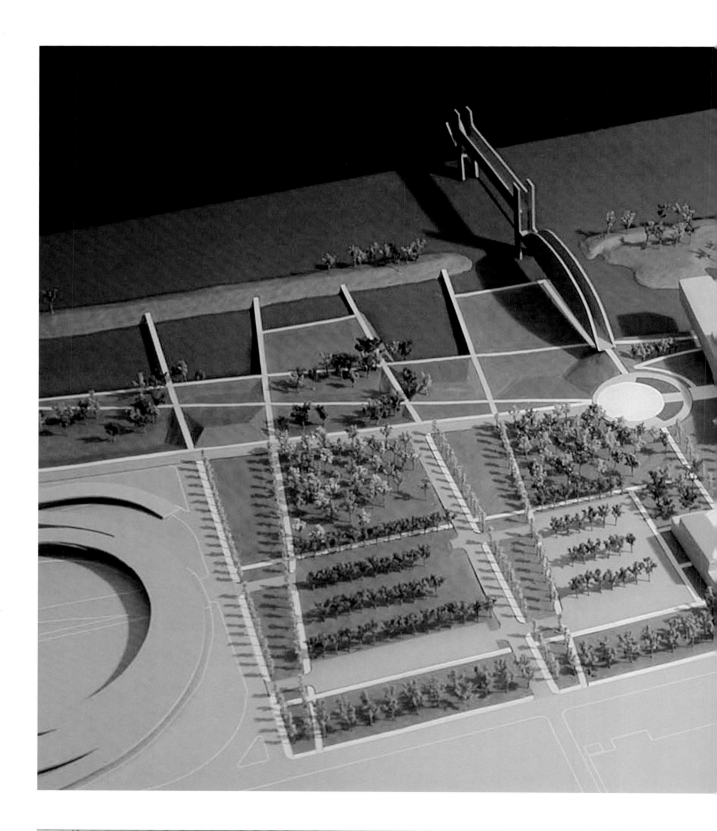

FIGURE 145. The clay model shows the intended extension of the gridded pathways over the wetland (top left), where the zones between the paths would have alternated between lawn and wetland.

FIGURE 146. Facing west, one sees the rows of holly
alternating with the maples as their colors begin to turn.
Image courtesy of Tim Hursley.

FIGURE 147. The east side of the building was originally intended to have tall grasses and meadow, alternating with lawn. The owner left it as lawn due to its success during large events (as seen in this image). On the ground during nonevents, however the space is static, greatly contrasting with the west side of the building. Image courtesy of Tim Hursley.

FIGURE 148. A close-up grading plan of the areas shown in
the following images (the top half was not built according to
Hargreaves' design). Redrawn by Keith VanDerSys based on
information provided by Hargreaves Associates.

FIGURE 149. The ridge of President Clinton Avenue leads
to the building entrance. The faceted topography is situated
between this ridge and the newly constructed wetland.
Photograph by the author.

FIGURE 150. As with many of Hargreaves's projects, the
topography beckons movement such as running, rolling, and
sledding. Photograph by the author.

FIGURE 151. The different slopes that occur on either side of the path are visible in this photograph, as one looks northwest from the central path up to the ridge. Photograph by the author.

AFTERWORD

THE EXTENSIVE PARK AND PARKWAY BUILDING THAT TOOK PLACE IN THE UNITED STATES IN THE LATE NINETEENTH AND EARLY TWENTIETH CENTURIES HAPPENED DURING MAJOR TRANSFORMATIONS IN INDUSTRY, ECONOMY, AND ATTENDANT URBANIZATION.

For mid-twentieth-century modernists, landscape design was largely rooted in the rise of corporate America, the postwar housing boom, and the creation of urban plazas. Today, landscape architects again find themselves with large, public commissions, but operating within radically different socioeconomic contexts and site conditions. Elizabeth Meyer has noted the importance of geology for those of Olmsted's day; the sites they dealt with had "sectional form, structure, depth and content."[1] Today, the traces of deep time in remnant sites are rarely visible and the physical armature in support of a site's structure and depth—soil, topography—must be manufactured to an even greater degree than in the past. This book has described the various ways that Hargreaves Associates has approached this challenge of fabricating ground, ways that foreground the relationship between form and process at different scales, from geographies (how to recover sites in the spaces that economic processes have literally and figuratively leveled) to techniques (how the tectonics of landscape express an affiliation be-

tween human-made forms and natural processes, especially in the context of "sustainability," which is itself formless), to effects (how working the ground by means of varied topography is an essential craft for transforming leveled sites into dynamic, public spaces). Hargreaves not only responded to the greater shifts in sensibility of the post–Earth Day era but continues to define how these shifts are manifest in landscapes in compelling ways. With a practice spanning three decades, Hargreaves Associates' work offers a window into this dramatic transformation of site, and makes evident that the significant and expressive aspects of landscape should not be discounted as more and more practical demands are placed on landscapes.

To the three E's of sustainability (equity, environment, and economics) has been added a fourth: energy. With global warming, rising tides, dependence on non-renewable energy sources, and growing concerns over food security—all systemic issues—landscapes in general, and parks in particular, are increasingly seen as productive grounds to specifically address these issues. This will surely lead to changes in how such landscapes look and function. In design competitions and landscape architecture schools, there is nary an image that is not teeming with wildlife, solar panels, windmills, constructed wetlands, and urban farms. Park competition briefs, such as those for Downsview Park Toronto and Orange County Great Park, request that projects promote energy-saving technologies and produce their own energy on site. The various Olympic venues, beginning with Sydney in 2000 and including London in 2012, whose major public spaces are also designed by Hargreaves Associates, have been making progress toward these goals.[2]

The 2012 Olympics is a colossal undertaking involving huge teams of consultants to oversee major redevelopment, rebuilding of transit infrastructure, and a massive effort to cleanse toxins and recycle most materials on site. The planning of the landscape includes a biodiversity action plan and the site is designed to provide over one hundred acres of habitat comprised of woodlands, constructed wetlands, reedbeds, and meadows. Specialists working on the project included researchers (horticulturalists and ecologists) who developed special seed mixtures for creating the meadows. The massive sculpted landforms designed by Hargreaves Associates are made from on-site soil that was decontaminated using sorting and washing machines, and microorganisms that neutralize the pollutants. The technologies and techniques tested here—and

FIGURE 152. The Byxbee Park field of poles was assumed to shift over time, an index of the settling trash below. Image courtesy of Jitze Couperus.

used on such a large scale—will likely become common practice for future developments.

Notwithstanding the fact that selling the green games cannot be separated from the corporatization of the Olympics (and notwithstanding the irony that "sustainability partners" include BP and Dow Chemical), the establishment of the transit and public space infrastructure will far outlast the Games and will likely become as integral to the fabric and life of the city as have London's historic parks.[3] As important, the particular forms, materials, and the privileging of certain types of habitat determine the character of the place and indicate which environmental and social characteristics are valued at this particular moment, as well as reveal the inevitably conflicting ideals inherent in such undertakings (i.e., Dow funding and frog habitat creation).[4]

This centrality of design makes it important to remember where the discipline was three decades ago when Hargreaves criticized his predecessors for the limitations of the functional diagram that resulted in a plethora of information useful for planning purposes but which was unable to give specificity and form to this information. We will end up in the same stalemate if we pit the compositional against the procedural, or the aesthetic against the functional, or confuse openness with lack of formal

FIGURE 153. The field of poles seen in this drawing for Governors Island is made up of windmills, marking a shift in priorities from objects that simply register change to icons of a productive landscape and energy infrastructure.

and material precision. An emphasis on the economic and infrastructural agency of landscape should not be detached from its experiential, imaginative, and experimental aspects. These wide-ranging concerns were inseparable for our predecessors, who worked across spatial scales, and they should remain so today if we are to engage the full range of landscape architecture's efficacy.

FIGURE 154. The wetland during construction at the north end of London Olympic Park can be seen in the foreground. The topography was made using the remediated soil. Over 80 percent of the 1.4 million cubic meters of contaminated soil was cleaned for reuse on the site. © ODA 2008, photograph taken February 11, 2008, by Anthony Charlton.

OPPOSITE

FIGURE 155. The wetland after construction. Image courtesy of Hargreaves Associates and LDA.

FIGURE 156. The reconstructed river's edge can be seen in the foreground of the large earthworks. Photo taken from the north area of the Parklands, looking south toward Olympic Stadium. © ODA 2008, photograph taken September 14, 2011, by Anthony Charlton.

PROJECT TEAMS FOR CITED PROJECTS

BRIGHTWATER WASTEWATER TREATMENT PLANT AND NORTHERN MITIGATION AREA

Snohomish County, Washington, 2004–11
Client: King County
Size: 114 acres
Engineer: CH2M HILL and Brown & Caldwell
Salmon Habitat: Daley Design
Environmental Consulting: 2020 Engineering
Education and Interpretive Systems: Lehrman
Cameron Studio
Artists: Jann Rosen-Queralt, Buster Simpson and
Ellen Sollod

BYXBEE PARK

Palo Alto, California, 1988–91
Client: City of Palo Alto
Size: Master plan: 150 acres; phase 1: 35 acres
Artist: Peter Richards, Michael Oppenheimer
Architect: Davis Davis Architects

CANDLESTICK POINT PARK

State Recreation Area, San Francisco, California
1985–91
Client: State of California Parks and Recreation
Size: 18 acres
Architect: MACK Architects
Artist: Doug Hollis

CRISSY FIELD

San Francisco, California, 1994–2001
Client: Golden Gate National Parks Association
Size: 100 acres
Wetland Hydrologic Design: Philip Williams &
Associates
Civil Engineer: Moffatt & Nichol Engineers
Habitat Biologist: Wetland Research Associates
Architect: Tanner Leddy Maytum Stacy

GUADALUPE RIVER PARK

San Jose, California, 1988–99
Client: San Jose Redevelopment Agency, Santa
Clara Valley Water District, U.S. Army Corps
of Engineers
Size: 50 acres
Civil and Hydrological Engineer: AN West, Inc.
Geotechnical Engineer: AGS, Inc.
Ecological and Environmental Planning: H. T.
Harvey and Associates

LONDON OLYMPICS 2012

London, England, 2008–12
Client: Olympic Delivery Authority
Size: 252 acres
Executive Landscape Architect: LDA Design
Planting Design: Nigel Dunnett and James
Hitchmough with Sarah Price, LDA Design
and Hargreaves Associates

LOS ANGELES STATE HISTORIC PARK

Los Angeles, California, 2006–8

Client: California State Parks

Size: 32 acres

Architect: Michael Maltzan Architecture

Interpretive Planner: Ralph Applebaum Associates

Associate Landscape Architect: Katherine Spitz
   Associates

Associate Urban Design: Arthur Golding

LOUISVILLE WATERFRONT PARK

Louisville, Kentucky, 1990–2008

Client: Waterfront Development Corporation

Size: Master plan: 120 acres; phase 1: 55 acres;
   phase 2: 17 acres; phase 3: 13 acres

Architect: Bravura Corporation

Fountain Engineer: Dan Euser Waterarchitecture

Architect: Tanner Leddy Maytum Stacy

SYDNEY OLYMPICS 2000

Sydney, Australia, 1996–2000

Client: Olympic Coordination Authority

Size: Master plan: 640 acres; plaza and water
   features: 31.5 acres

Associate Architects: Government Architect
   Design Directorate, Schaffer Barnsley, Anton
   James, Gavin McMillian

Architect: Tonkin Zulaikha Greer

Fountain Engineer: Sydney Fountains Waterforms

**21ST CENTURY WATERFRONT AND
RENAISSANCE PARKS**

Chattanooga, Tennessee, 2002–5

Client: RiverCity Company

Size: Master plan: 129 acres; phase 1: 63 acres

Associate Architect (master plan phase): Schwartz/
   Silver Architects

Artists: James Carpentar, Gadugi Team

Fountain Engineer: Dan Euser Waterarchitecture

Renaissance Park: 23 acres

Architect (Renaissance Park):
   Eskew+Dumez+Ripple

**UNIVERSITY OF CINCINNATI MASTER PLAN
AND AFFILIATED PROJECTS**

Cincinnati, Ohio (1989–2006)

Client: University of Cincinnati

Size: Master plan, 200 acres

Main Street: 8.48 acres, 2000–2005

Architect: Gwathmey Siegel & Associates
   Architects, Moore Ruble Yudell Architects &
   Planners, Morphosis

Associate Architects: Glaserworks, KZF Design,
   GBBN architects

Sigma Sigma Commons: 3.4 acres, 1995–98

Tower Architect: Machado and Silvetti Associates

Campus Green: 2.7 acres, 1997–2000

Fountain Engineer: Dan Euser Waterarchitecture

**WILLIAM J. CLINTON PRESIDENTIAL CENTER
PARK**

Little Rock, Arkansas, 2000–2005

Client: William J. Clinton Foundation

Size: 30 acres

Architect: Polshek Partnership Architects

Associate Landscape Architect: Landscape
   Architecture Inc.

Fountain Engineer: Dan Euser Waterarchitecture

NOTES

PREFACE

1   Charles Waldheim, who coined the phrase "landscape urbanism," founded a concentration of landscape urbanism (now defunct) within the school of architecture at the University of Illinois, Chicago. He is now chair of landscape architecture at Harvard Graduate School of Design. Mohsen Mostafavi, now dean of Harvard Graduate School of Design, was involved in founding the postgraduate certificate in landscape urbanism at the Architectural Association and is editor, with Ciro Najle, of *Landscape Urbanism: A Manual for the Machinic Landscape* (London: Architectural Association, 2003); though this version of landscape urbanism is quite distinct from its North American counterpart in methodology. Though there have been further efforts to expand the theoretical and historical terrain of Landscape Urbanism (see Dean Almy, ed., *Center 14: On Landscape Urbanism* [Austin: Center for American Architecture and Design, 2007]), its definition in the North American context is largely affiliated with the Harvard Graduate School of Design (because of Waldheim and Mostafavi) and the University of Pennsylvania, because of James Corner's affiliation with the term.

2   Introduction to Hargreaves et al., *Landscape Alchemy: The Work of Hargreaves Associates* (Pt. Reyes Station, Calif.: ORO Editions, 2009), 6. This statement is true of the firm's public projects. Some earlier corporate plazas or residential projects, of which it has designed only a handful, were not brownfield sites.

3   This scale has been unfavorably referred to as "decorative." As noted by Charles Waldheim when referring to the work of West 8, landscape urbanism deemphasizes "the middle scale of decorative or architectural work and [favors] instead the large-scale infrastructural diagram and the small-scale material condition." See "Landscape as Urbanism," in Waldheim, ed., *The Landscape Urbanism Reader* (New York: Princeton Architectural Press, 2006), 45.

4   This characterization of the work was described by George Hargreaves in an interview with the author, and is supported by a comparative reading of two collections of the firm's work. The first collection was edited by Steve Hanson, who was Hargreaves's employee at the time. See Hanson, ed., "Hargreaves: Landscape Works," *Process Architecture* 128 (January 1996). The latest compilation is *Landscape Alchemy*, a book-length monograph containing thirty-four projects. Both publications include essays by critics offering interpretations of the firm's work.

INTRODUCTION

1 Charles Jencks, *The Language of Post-Modern Architecture* (New York: Rizzoli, 1977), 9.

2 Elizabeth K. Meyer, "The Post–Earth Day Conundrum: Translating Environmental Values into Landscape Design," in Michel Conan, ed., *Environmentalism in Landscape Architecture* (Washington, D.C.: Dumbarton Oaks, 2000).

3 This phrase "shift in sensibility" is borrowed from David Harvey (after Andreas Huyssen), who characterizes the shift from modernism to postmodernism as a change in sensibility. David Harvey, "Postmodernism," in *The Condition of Postmodernity: An Enquiry into the Origins of Cultural Change* (Cambridge: Basil Blackwell, 1992), 39.

4 Roland Barthes, "The Death of the Author," in *Image, Music, Text* (New York: Hill and Wang, 1977), 142–148, and Umberto Eco, *The Open Work* (Cambridge, Mass.: Harvard University Press, 1989).

5 Rosalind E. Krauss, "Sculpture in the Expanded Field," in *The Originality of the Avant-Garde and Other Modernist Myths* (Cambridge, Mass.: MIT Press, 1985). As Krauss emphasizes in the introduction to her book, "method is what criticism is"; there is no understanding of a work outside method because any interpretations are in fact only a "product of what a given method allows one to ask or even to think of asking" (5).

6 Hargreaves's major early influences were artists such as Robert Smithson and Richard Serra. See John Beardsley, "Poet of Landscape Process," *Landscape Architecture* 85:12 (December 1995): 46–51, quote on 48. For an essay that discusses Hargreaves Associates' work directly in relation to notions of "textuality" and "contextuality," see Rossana Vaccarino, "I paesaggi ri-fatti = Re-made landscapes," *Lotus international* 87 (1995): 82–107.

7 See Meyer, "The Post–Earth Day Conundrum." Also see Anne Whiston Spirn, "The Poetics of City and Nature: Towards a New Aesthetic for Urban Design," *Landscape Journal* 7:10 (1988): 108–126; Catherine Howett, "Systems, Signs, Sensibilities: Sources for a New Landscape Aesthetic," *Landscape Journal* 6:1 (1987): 1–12; and Robert Thayer, "Visual Ecology: Revitalizing the Aesthetics of Landscape Architecture," *Landscape* 20:2 (1976): 37–43.

8 For an explication of various practitioners who attempted to bridge this divide, including Hargreaves, Michael Van Valkenburgh, and Laurie Olin, see Meyer, "The Post–Earth Day Conundrum." For her description of the "divide," see 187–188.

9 See Fritjof Capra, "Systems Theory and the New Paradigm," in Carolyn Merchant, ed., *Ecology* (Atlantic Highlands, N.J.: Humanities Press, 1994). Also see Ilya Prigogine, *From Being to Becoming: Time and Complexity in the Physical Sciences* (San Francisco: W. H. Freeman, 1980). More recently, see Kristina Hill, "Shifting Sites," in Carol J. Burns and Andrea Kahn, eds., *Site Matters: Design Concepts, Histories, and Strategies* (New York: Routledge, 2005).

10 References to ecology and biology as models for design are too numerous to cite but can be seen in a wide-ranging body of work, from Stan Allen's "Artificial Ecologies: The Work of MVRDV," *El Croquis* 86 (1997): 26–33, to Manual DeLanda's "Deleuze and the Use of the Genetic Algorithm in Architecture," in *Phylogenesis: FOA's Ark* (Barcelona: Actar, 2003), and Greg Lynn's *Animate Form* (New York: Princeton

Architectural Press, 1999). Also see landscape architect James Corner's "Ecology and Landscape as Agents of Creativity," in George F. Thompson and Frederick R. Steiner, eds., *Ecological Design and Planning* (New York: John Wiley & Sons, 1997). This broad array of interpretations is especially visible in architecture. As one critic comments, "An enormous gulf exists between those who look to the new model of nature as the source of new generative strategies and/or forms and those who look to it as the source of new ways of constructing and running buildings." See Susannah Hagan, "Five Reasons (To Adopt Environmental Design)," in William S. Saunders, ed., *Nature, Landscape, and Building for Sustainability: A Harvard Design Magazine Reader* (Minneapolis: University of Minnesota Press, 2008), 100–113. Quote on 103. Also see Conan, Introduction to *Environmentalism in Landscape Architecture*.

11 See J. William Thompson, "After Vision Reflection," *Landscape Architecture* 81:12 (December 1991): 55. However, in other instances, Hargreaves has used terminology such as "open-ended compositions" or "expressing the processes of nature through open-ended vehicles of culture." See George Hargreaves, "Most Influential Landscapes," *Landscape Journal* 12:2 (Fall 1993): 177.

12 For example, see Mohsen Mostafavi and Ciro Najle, eds., *Landscape Urbanism: A Manual for the Machinic Landscape* (London: Architectural Association, 2003). Mostafavi asserts that "landscape urbanism will in future, with its temporal and political characteristics, set the scene (albeit momentary) for democracy in action" (9).

13 Charles Waldheim is referring to Amsterdam's Schiphol Airport by West 8 in "Landscape as Urbanism," in Waldheim, ed., *The Landscape Urbanism Reader* (New York: Princeton Architectural Press, 2006), 46.

14 Schwartz does not name Hargreaves Associates directly but uses an image of its Louisville Waterfront Park as an example. See "Respondents," *Harvard Design Magazine* 20 (Spring–Summer 2004): 27, 28, 43.

15 George Hargreaves, interview with author, May 26, 2005.

16 See "Discussions with Heizer, Oppenheim, Smithson [1970]," in Jack Flam, ed., *Robert Smithson: The Collected Writings* (Berkeley: University of California Press, 1996), 250.

17 See Meyer, "The Post–Earth Day Conundrum."

18 See James Corner, "The Agency of Mapping: Speculation, Critique and Invention," in Denis Cosgrove, ed., *Mappings* (London: Reaktion Books, 1999). Also see the work of Anuradha Mathur and Dilip da Cunha.

19 Hargreaves, drawing on Robert Irwin, refers to the importance of these terms in his essay "Post-Modernism Looks beyond Itself," *Landscape Architecture* (July 1983): 62–63. The introduction to Hargreaves Associates' work in Steve Hanson, ed., "Hargreaves: Landscape Works," *Process Architecture* 128 (January, 1996), is by Susan Rademacher and is titled "Toward Site Specificity." The "site-specific" in reference to Hargreaves Associates' work is also used by Julia Czerniak, "Looking Back at Landscape Urbanism: Speculations on Site," in Waldheim, *The Landscape Urbanism Reader*. And "site-generated" is one of the key terms employed by Anita Berrizbeitia in "Key Words and Phrases," in George Hargreaves et al., *Landscape Alchemy: The Work of Hargreaves Associates* (Pt. Reyes Station, Calif.: ORO Editions, 2009). Berrizbeitia, like Czerniak, refers to Robert Irwin's discussion of varying degrees of engagement

7   Pope, *Ladders*, 239. Pope is referring, in particular, to the leapfrogging checkerboard pattern of gated communities that creates private enclaves separated by "open space."

8   The version of landscape urbanism as laid out by Charles Waldheim is positioned directly against New Urbanism. For a recent piece on the conflict between leading proponents of both camps, see the *Boston Globe* article "Green Building" by Leon Neyfakh published online January 30, 2011, http://www.boston.com/bostonglobe/ideas/articles/2011/01/30/green_building/?page=full, accessed February 5, 2011

9   Harvey, Megacities Lecture 4, 37.

10 Pope, *Ladders*, 214.

11 For example, for the projects focused on in this chapter, Hargreaves Associates' four-year involvement for the 129-acre Chattanooga 21st-Century Waterfront Plan was preceded by twenty years of community participation and development. Similarly, Crissy Field required fifty public meetings during design development; and the designation of Los Angeles State Historic Park is the result of years of community activism to keep the site available for public use.

12 Harvey, Megacities Lecture 4, 78.

13 I borrow the phrase "principle of acknowledgement" from Craig Owens because it is useful to describe Hargreaves Associates' approach to history. Owens asserts that "the activism of modernism was an attempt to substitute a principle of *acknowledgement* of the past for the passive adaptation of traditional forms." Owens's reference to modernism uses particular building examples and should not be confused with large-scale master planning, critiqued earlier. Craig Owens, "Philip Johnson: History, Genealogy, Historicism," in David Whitney and Jeffrey Kipnis, eds., *Philip Johnson: The Glass House* (New York: Pantheon Books, 1993), 88. This essay was originally published in 1978.

14 The quote is from George Hargreaves, "Post Modernism Looks Beyond Itself," *Landscape Architecture* 73:4 (July–August 1983): 65. In this essay Hargreaves cites a wide range of practices, from Venturi and Scott Brown to Frank Gehry to Martha Schwartz.

15 George Hargreaves, "Large Parks: A Designer's Perspective," in Julia Czerniak and George Hargreaves, eds., *Large Parks* (New York: Princeton Architectural Press, 2007), 169.

16 George Hargreaves et al., *Landscape Alchemy: The Work of Hargreaves Associates* (Pt. Reyes Station, Calif.: ORO Editions, 2009), 6.

17 The start dates for these projects (Candlestick 1985, Byxbee 1988) are consistent across publications; however the "end" dates when construction is completed are inconsistent even between Hargreaves's first compilation, Steve Hanson, ed., "Hargreaves: Landscape Works," *Process: Architecture* 128 (1996), and the recent *Landscape Alchemy*. The dates used here are based on the dates given to me by the managers of the respective parks, even though these dates were also stated as tentative.

18 For a further discussion of this project as well as Guadalupe River Park and Plaza Park in San Jose, see Julia Czerniak, "Looking Back at Landscape Urbanism," in Waldheim, *The Landscape Urbanism Reader*, 105–123.

19 George Hargreaves has used the word "narrative" interchangeably with "metaphor" and "allegory" to refer to those aspects of the work that are allusive. See Reuben Rainey, "'Physicality' and 'Narrative': The Urban Parks of Hargreaves Associates," *Process: Architecture* 128 (1996): 29–44.

20 Hargreaves is referencing Parc du Sausset by Michel and Claire Corajoud. He goes on to say that the available onsite education gives park-goers the opportunity "to learn of the landscape's deeper meaning [which] is a plus." Hargreaves, "Large Parks," 158.

21 Hargreaves et al., *Landscape Alchemy*, p. 8.

22 Bella Dicks, *Culture on Display: The Production of Contemporary Visitability* (Maidenhead, England: Open University Press, 2003), 73. See the introduction and ch. 2, "Cities on Display," for how use of symbolism pertains to this discussion on legibility.

23 Dicks, *Culture on Display*, 36. On place promotion, see 73. Her examples include waterfront developments such as Cardiff Bay and the Millennium Dome.

24 See ch. 4, "Memory and Emotion," in Susan Herrington, *On Landscapes* (New York: Routledge, 2009).

25 Hargreaves, "Large Parks," 165. Hargreaves's primary criticism of Latz's park design in Duisburg Nord is the lack of an interpretive program that would explain that Jewish slave laborers were forced to work there to further the Nazi war machine.

26 This is not to say that fragments and remnants are mutually exclusive since actual remnants can be combined to make a new fragment. This distinction was noted by John Dixon Hunt in conversation with the author, March 4, 2009.

27 Bernard Tschumi, *Cinegramme Folie le Parc de la Villette* (New York: Princeton Architectural Press, 1987), 2, 24.

28 Sanford Kwinter, *Architectures of Time* (Cambridge, Mass.: MIT Press, 2002), 38.

29 The tidal marsh at Crissy Field took one year to make, half of which was spent excavating 227,000 tons of fill, much of it contaminated. The placement of its inlet initially caused the adjacent beach to lose twenty-five feet of its width due to the changed wave action, upsetting surfers and almost destroying the new promenade. It took two years after implementing a solution for the beach to stabilize. For an account of the engineering challenges of Crissy Field, see Brad Porter, "Transforming Crissy Field," *Civil Engineering* (March 2003): 38–45.

30 *Crissy Field Restoration Project Summary of Monitoring Data 2000–2004*, report by the National Park Service, U.S. Department of the Interior, Golden Gate National Recreation Area, January 2006, 31, http://www.californiawetlands.net/upfiles/4282/CrissyField_MonitoringReport.pdf, accessed April 5, 2008. Also see the *Crissy Field Marsh Expansion Study Final Report*, Philip Williams & Associates, March 16, 2004, http://library.presidio.gov/archive/documents/CrissyField_Exp_Chpt_1%20to%203_accesible.pdf, accessed April 5, 2008.

31 The Williams report states that "the system appears to be in dynamic equilibrium, with the marsh presently in its transitional state as a mesotidal sandy coastal lagoon. Based on the limited amount of estuarine sedimentation data to date, we expect the site to maintain its present condition as an open water lagoon subject to intermittent closures for several decades." *Crissy Field Marsh Expansion Study Final Report*, 2.

32 Andreas Huyssen, *Present Pasts: Urban Palimpsests and the Politics of Memory* (Stanford, Calif.: Stanford University Press, 2003), 5. Though Huyssen's book deals largely with memory pertaining to war, especially actual sites of destruction such as the Berlin Wall, the Holocaust Museum, or the World Trade Center towers, his introduction more broadly pertains to questions about cultural memory in lived space.

33 They were relocated in 1838 as a result of the Indian Removal Act of 1830. The trail is known in Cherokee as the "Trail where they cried."

34 Ross's Landing is named after John Ross, the city's founder and later principal chief of the Cherokee nation for thirty-eight years.

35 Team Gadugi, as the group of artists is called, produced the artworks for the Trail of Tears at Ross's Landing. The artists are Gary Allen, Wade Bennett, Ken Foster, Bill Glass, Demos Glass, and Robby McMurtry.

36 Glass says that "this is so much more than a memorial. It is a physical celebration of our Cherokee culture. It is important to us to reconnect with this community and come full circle in this journey." See Dan Agent, "Cherokee monumental art returns to origins," at Cherokeephoenix.org, http://www.cherokeephoenix.org/18486/Article.aspx, accessed October 26, 2011.

37 See Dicks, *Culture on Display*, 133–134, for her distinction between history and heritage. She considers heritage as "history made visitable" in that it is produced within the cultural economy of visitability (tourism) but centered on local cultures and personal stories. Dicks also notes, "green spaces have had to enter the economy of signs in order to survive under market conditions. Or, to put it another way, changing market conditions have made them into an economic asset that can signify a new era" (116).

38 The Central Park Conservancy, established in 1980, is an early and economically successful model. For a criticism of lack of governmental funding for parks, see Patrick Arden, "The High Cost of Free Parks," *Next American City* 27 (Summer 2010), http://americancity.org/magazine/article/the-high-cost-of-free-parks/, accessed September 7, 2010. The flip side of Arden's criticism is that the immense funds that a city would pay to places like Central Park can instead be spent on other parks.

39 Hargreaves is referring to Sydney's Centennial Parklands, where its heritage status is freezing it in a particular moment and not letting it evolve based on new needs. Hargreaves, "Large Parks," 146.

40 The site is celebrated for its importance to agriculture since part of the first irrigation canal to bring water from the Los Angeles river to the Pueblo de Los Angeles, the Zanja Madre, built in the late 1700s, passes near it; and the site was used for over 120 years by the Southern Pacific Railroad, which enabled California to become a major exporter of agricultural goods. The area has long been a site of contestation and injustice, including violence against Indians and Hispanics in the mid-nineteenth century, the Chinatown Massacre in 1871, the relocation of Japanese Americans during World War II, the demolition of the original Chinatown in 1933 to build Union Station, the severing of Solano Canyon and Elysian Park by the Pasadena Freeway, and the forced relocation of the Chavez Ravine community for what became Dodger Stadium.

41 The primary themes have two subthemes each: Flow of History is subdivided into "A People's History" and "History of Place," and Environmental Justice is subdivided into "Water" and "Environmental Actions." This information was gathered from "Los Angeles State Historic Park Interpretive Master Plan Final Draft," August 23, 2006, unpublished manuscript, provided to me by Hargreaves Associates for reference.

42 One of Hargreaves Associates' consultants, who were also part of the competition team, is exhibition designer Ralph Appelbaum Associates.

43 The Chinatown Yard Alliance is a group of individuals from the surrounding community and businesses. FoLAR had already been actively looking at the area for its

redevelopment potential, though it did not have in mind a historic state park. In 1998, the organization and the University of Southern California's School of Architecture launched a series of design sessions in the adjacent neighborhoods and sponsored a conference called "River through Downtown." The proposed design was a mixed-use plan that included housing, commercial and retail space, a park, a school, and a "canal" as on ode to the Zanja Madre. The Urban and Environment Policy Institute at Occidental College sponsored a yearlong series of programs called "Re-Envisioning the Los Angeles River: A Program of Community and Ecological Revitalization" (1999–2000) and the University of California at Los Angeles's Department of Urban Planning produced a report titled *Cornfield of Dreams: A Resource Guide of Facts, Issues and Principles* (2000) on the historical and planning issues that affect the site.

44   *Los Angeles State Historic Park General Plan and Final Environmental Impact Report*, approved by the State Parks and Recreation Commission, June 10, 2005, 61–62.

45   The Center for Law in the Public Interest is a nonprofit law firm that represents traditionally underrepresented people and organizations. See Robert Garcia, Erica S. Flores, and Elizabeth Pine, *Dreams of Fields: Soccer, Community, and Equal Justice* (Santa Monica, Calif.: Center for Law in the Public Interest, 2002), 24, http://www.cityprojectca.org/pdf/dreamsoffields.pdf, accessed June 9, 2012. The same organization issued a report in 2004—*The Cornfield and the Flow of History: People, Place, and Culture*—recommending a "minimal built-out option" for the site that would maximize the amount of open space for recreation and not allow museums and buildings to be constructed.

46   Upon purchase of the site by the state in 2000, the Cornfield State Park Advisory Committee was formed, a thirty-six-member unit comprising individuals with local, regional, and statewide perspectives, in an attempt to bring the various issues to the forefront. In producing its report, *A Unified Vision for Cornfield State Park* (2003) the committee invited George Hargreaves, then chair of Harvard's Landscape Architecture program, to speak as an outside expert regarding the issues facing the creation of the park. According to the report, Hargreaves recommended that the group develop a visionary sense for the place, as an "organic whole" rather than a patchwork of "balkanized" spaces, and that it keep in mind the capacity of the relatively small site. As with LASHP and Crissy Field, Louisville Waterfront Park does not allow formally designated recreational zones for the same reasons. The president of the Waterfront Development Corporation, David Karem, says that allowing space to be dominated by one specific group (for instance, one soccer field) makes it impossible to say "no" to any other group that wants its own space. Karem, interview with author, September 30, 2011.

47   Hargreaves Associates looked at funding and governance structures for the park. A full one-third of the schematic design fee went to this end. Working with the firm's consultant, Economic Research Associates, Hargreaves Associates prepared an economic analysis based on projected visitation rates, program revenue, and maintenance costs in an attempt to balance the financial realities of the park with flexible use so that it does not become an entirely revenue-generating landscape, hence privatized and exclusive. Hargreaves Associates employee, interview with author, August 27, 2008.

48 Owens, "Philip Johnson," 82.

49 Hargreaves, "Large Parks," 150. Though he is referring in this particular essay to sites greater than five hundred acres, this approach can be seen in the projects throughout this book, all of which are less than two hundred acres.

50 Hargreaves, "Large Parks," 171.

51 J. William Thompson, "Field of Vision," *Landscape Architecture* 87:7 (July 1997): 39, quoting Michael Boland from Golden Gate National Parks Association, who said that the plan "doesn't look as if a turf war was fought here. . . . I think of the plan as a tapestry—a political as well as a design document."

CHAPTER 2. TECHNIQUES

Notes to epigraphs: John Brinckerhoff Jackson, *Discovering the Vernacular Landscape* (New Haven, Conn.: Yale University Press, 1984), 8; Garrett Eckbo, *Landscape for Living* (Santa Monica, Calif.: Hennessey + Ingalls, 2002), 59.

1 Raymond Williams, *Keywords: A Vocabulary of Culture and Society*, rev. ed. (New York: Oxford University Press, 1983), 315.

2 For example, LEED (Leadership in Energy and Environmental Design) is a certification system for buildings and includes provisions for sites. While laudable in its goals of reducing resource use and looking at the long-term costs of buildings, its point system is far too generic, leading to a checklist of single treatments rather than a comprehensive approach that considers the local context, climate, and project specifics. The Sustainable Sites Initiative is the equivalent for site design and is much more comprehensive than the site criteria in LEED. Both are voluntary programs.

3 "Function" can mean any purpose for which something is designed, whether for a quantifiable task, a symbolic task, or a program of any type. In this chapter, "function" is used to refer to specific and quantifiable tasks, such as water collection, whereas the term "program" is used to refer to more varied social uses. These terms are not exclusive of each other; for example, a surface can be designed to function as a water collection system (meaning that its size and detailing respond to this criterion), but it can be programmed to support any number of activities.

4 George Hargreaves et al., *Landscape Alchemy: The Work of Hargreaves Associates* (Pt. Reyes Station, Calif., ORO Editions, 2009), 8.

5 See, respectively, Liz Campbell Kelly, "A Maximal Practice," 288, 290, and Anita Berrizbeitia, "Key Words and Phrases," 64, in Hargreaves et al., *Landscape Alchemy*. The attitude expressed in these various essays is similar to what Elizabeth K. Meyer refers to as the "yawners" (sustainability is inherent to landscape architecture, so what is the big deal?) or the "disdainers," for which she uses Hargreaves, among others, as an example. Meyer defines "disdainers" as those who downplay sustainability in public even though they adopt it in practice. Meyer also mentions Julie Bargmann, Michael VanValkenburgh, and the "self-identified landscape urbanists" such as James Corner, Charles Waldheim, and Chris Reed. She does, however, use Crissy Field by Hargreaves Associates as an example that offers a productive alliance among all definitions of sustainability. See Meyer, "Sustaining Beauty: The Performance of Appearance," *Journal of Landscape Architecture* (Spring 2008): 30–47.

6   Intermediate projects, such as Louisville Waterfront Park, would not be considered sustainable if judged by measures of potable water consumption and reuse, or stormwater treatment (there is none). Though there is recycling of fountain water, restrictions regarding human contact prohibit many fountains from using stormwater runoff unless it has been treated to a level that is often cost or space prohibitive for individual water features.

7   Lewis Mumford, well known for his work on cities and regional planning, wrote the first comprehensive study on the history of technology, *Technics and Civilization*, in 1934. He critiques the doctrine of progress, which puts ultimate faith in technology as the driving force of human improvement and results in all-encompassing systems that have detached us from nature and deprived us of aesthetic, meaningful engagement with technology. See Lewis Mumford, *Technics and Civilization* (New York: Harcourt, Brace & World, 1963). His definition of polytechnics can be found in his later work, *The Myth of the Machine: Technics and Human Development* (New York: Harcourt, Brace & World, 1967), 255.

8   Ivan Illich, *H₂0 and the Waters of Forgetfulness* (London: Marion Boyars, 1986), 75, 76.

9   Carolyn Merchant, *The Columbia Guide to American Environmental History* (New York: Columbia University Press, 2002), 174–175.

10   Even though there were earlier regulations, the umbrella agency to oversee these controls—the Environmental Protection Agency (EPA)—was not created until 1970. For an excellent description of how this shift to environmentalism was marked by reforming administrative accountability, see ch. 11, "The Rise of Modern Environmentalism," in Richard N. L. Andrews, *Managing the Environment, Managing Ourselves: A History of American Environmental Policy* (New Haven, Conn.: Yale University Press, 1999).

11   The Federal Water Pollution Control Act, passed in 1948, has been amended many times, each time with more stringent controls. A key revision in 1972—known as the Clean Water Act—established the standards for controlling point-source pollution, such as industrial and municipal sewage. It wasn't until 1987 that the Clean Water Act was expanded to include stormwater discharges at point sources (industrial and municipal), requiring permits for any discharges (National Pollutant Discharge Elimination System, or NPDES, phase 1). It also addressed nonpoint source pollution by establishing a grant program to expand research and development of nonpoint controls and management practices at local and state levels. Most measures to mitigate nonpoint source pollution occur at local, municipal levels. Of course, quantifications and regulations are not unbiased and can have unintended results. Recent regulations added to the Clean Water Act (phase 2 of NPDES, 1999), which include postconstruction water capture for sites over one acre, have been criticized because the stormwater regulations are calculated according to the ratio of building footprint to property area. This means an infill high-rise building built on existing impervious surface in a city gets a worse rating than an enormous single-family residence on a large, greenfield site. See Lisa Nisenson, "A Browner Shade of Green: The New Water Rules and the Next Chapter of Sprawl," *Landscape Architecture* 97:11 (November 2007): 122–124.

12   Stormwater that is piped along with household and industrial sewage (combined sewer systems) gets treated, yet adds significant volume to water pollution control plants, which often overflow during rainfall and dump untreated sewage directly into water bodies. And stormwater that is dealt with apart from other sewage (separate sewer systems) flows through pipes and enters the nearest water body untreated, risking more pollution. On-site collection helps with either type of sewer system.

13   Even though the best known, and apparently first, example of a constructed wetland for dealing with sewage is Frederick Law Olmsted's Fens and Riverway in Boston of the late nineteenth century, water pollution controls have been slow to advance. On Olmsted's project, see Anne Whiston Spirn, "Constructing Nature: The Legacy of Frederick Law Olmsted," in William Cronon, ed., *Uncommon Ground: Rethinking the Human Place in Nature* (New York: W. W. Norton, 1996), 91–113.

14   The Comprehensive Environmental Response, Compensation, and Liability Act (better known as Superfund, 1980) gave the EPA authority to sue polluters to clean up the most hazardous sites but also left those who weren't polluters—future owners and even lenders—liable for the cost of cleanup. See Rosanna Sattler et al., "New Designs in the Legal Landscape," in Niall Kirkwood, ed., *Manufactured Sites: Rethinking the Post-Industrial Landscape* (London: Taylor & Francis, 2001), 12. While Superfund pertains to the most hazardous sites in the country, the EPA launched its Brownfields Program in 1994 to address sites that have actual or perceived contamination and to help return sites to "productive use" through grants to developers.

15   Along with the Taxpayer Relief Act (1997) and the Small-Business Liability Relief Act (2002), costs associated with cleanup became tax deductible and grants became available. See Sattler et al., "New Designs in the Legal Landscape," 24-6.

16   George Hargreaves and Liz Campbell Kelly, "Interventions in Hydrology," TOPOS 59 (2007): 50–57, quote on 50.

17   The treatment pond was conceived to treat water from the adjacent sewage treatment plant; however, it was determined that this water could contain too many bacteria, thereby requiring that it be fenced off from human contact. This initial idea required multiple ponds for treatment, rather than the single pond of the final design; however, the figure of the ponds in relation to the adjacent landfill and creek is similar to the final design even though the function of the wetland radically changed. See Kevin Conger, "Sydney Olympics 2000: Northern Water Feature," in Kirkwood, *Manufactured Sites*, 221–238.

18   Again, because of possible contaminants, the wetland water is not used in the fountains. Scientists are doing postconstruction evaluations of Sydney Olympic Park to determine the success of its wetlands and treatment plant. The results to date show marked improvement in water quality within the park as compared to the water bodies outside it. Potable water was used in the fountains, as required by the Department of Health, until 2004. Once the water quality data was obtained, the Sydney Olympic Park Authority retrofitted the system so that the fountains now use recycled water after it is treated in the on-site treatment plant.

19   Hargreaves Associates serves as lead designer for the master plan phase, and the CH2M HILL engineering firm is the lead for construction contract delivery.

20　Brightwater is the most expensive water treatment plant built to date based on amount of sewage treated. The most appropriate site for the region's long-term needs was thirteen miles inland; it allowed for storage of wastewater during storms and the distribution of reclaimed water to four different cities, but also required the costs of piping the treated sewage to Puget Sound. Those residents who agreed to have the plant located near them wanted simultaneously to be sure that they were unaware of it (i.e., of the odor) and that it would provide an educational and recreational opportunity. Thus the public mitigation part of the project (odor control and habitat restoration) accounts for over 10 percent of the total project cost. See Donna Gordon Blankinship, "Bright Future at Brightwater," *Stormwater: The Journal for Surface Water Quality Professionals* (November–December 2004), http://www.stormh2o.com/november-december-2004/king-county-washington.aspx, accessed April 2, 2008.

21　Also near Seattle, the West Point Treatment Plant (1988–97) sits adjacent to a park. The designer, Danadjieva & Koenig Associates, expanded an existing facility by creating a dramatic, two-mile-long stepped planted wall, camouflaging the treatment plant. An article by Michael Leccese asserts that park users are oblivious to the working of the plant; however, Danadjieva, who worked with Lawrence Halprin on Seattle Freeway Park, designed the walkways along the planted wall so that at one point pedestrians are elevated above the walls and can see the treatment plant. See Leccese, "A Point Well Taken," *Landscape Architecture* 89:6 (June 1999): 62–69.

22　See the designer's website: Abel Bainnson Butz Landscape Architects, http://abbnyc.com/pdfs/all_downloads.pdf. To be fair, the large landforms along the western edge of Hargreaves Associates' design do block views from the road, but the valleys between them allow for syncopated views into the treatment plant area.

23　Tertiary treatment is often done with constructed wetlands for small projects. The necessity for tertiary treatment depends on the water body to which the effluent is directed or what the treated water will be used for. The Brightwater plant will not treat to tertiary levels and the plant treats too much waste for the landscape to handle it. Instead, "Brightwater will produce about 7 million gallons of Class A reclaimed water each day for on- and off-site uses, and eventually up to 21 million gallons per day as demand requires. The reclaimed water will also be used on-site for irrigation, tank cleaning, and other processes that do not require potable water." The remainder of the sewage is piped thirteen miles to outfall in Puget Sound. See King County "Wastewater Treatment," http://www.kingcounty.gov/environment/wtd/Construction/North/Brightwater/Description/Treatment-Plant.aspx, accessed April 2, 2008.

24　See Blankinship, paraphrasing Michael Popiwny, "Bright Future at Brightwater."

25　The second plan, by Royston Hanamoto Beck and Abey, was designed in the early 1970s based on the Model Cities Program. When the federal government cancelled the program in 1974, the project was cancelled. The Guadalupe River Task force was formed 1983 and it hired EDAW for the third plan, which apparently "fell victim to the disconnect between the Corps' design of major flood-control features along the river and the city's hope of inviting people to the water's edge." See the *Guadalupe River Park 2002 Master Plan* by the City of San Jose, the city's Redevelopment Authority, USACE, and Santa Clara Valley Water District, 36, http://www.grpg.org/

19   Bayer's project is in Kent, Washington. See C. Timothy Baird, "A Composed Ecology: After 20-Plus Years, How Is Herbert Bayer's Renowned Mill Creek Canyon Earthworks Holding Up?" *Landscape Architecture* 93:3 (2003): 68, 70–75, 89.

20   Unfortunately one row of holly was removed and the steps covered with a ramp of concrete to make room for construction equipment to access the wetland that was recently built.

21   The intense red plants in these areas are winter creeper, which is considered to be highly invasive in this region.

22   Luhmann, *Art as a Social System*, 23.

23   This latest turn to "affect," which eschews meaning altogether, is a noticeable trend in architecture; for example, see Robert E. Somol and Sarah Whiting, "Notes around the Doppler Effect and Other Moods of Modernism," *Perspecta* 33 (2002): 72–77. For an excellent overview of this turn in the humanities, which perfectly describes the sentiment in architecture, see Ruth Leys, "The Turn to Affect: A Critique," *Critical Inquiry* 37:3 (Spring 2011): 434–472, http://www.jstor.org/stable/10.1086/659353, accessed February 6, 2011. Leys points out that "the word *representation* is frequently used to refer to a picture of the relationship between the organism and the world that assumes a sharp separation between the cognizing, representing mind and its objects. This is a picture that the new affect theorists reject in favor of a more embodied account of mind-world interactions. . . . But the word *representation* is also used by the new affect theorists to refer to signification or meaning or belief, and so on, as if what is at stake in eschewing a representationalist theory of mind-world relations is not just a matter of rejecting a false picture of how mind and body interact but involves rejecting the role of signification, or cognition, or belief altogether. On this second usage, the claim becomes that, since we do not represent the world to ourselves according to the wrong, disembodied model of the mind, our relations to the world are, in large measure, visceral, embodied, and affective and hence not a matter of meaning or belief at all" (458–459, n. 43).

24   David K. Karem, president of the Louisville Waterfront Development Corporation, interview with author, September 30, 2011; and Jordan Johnson, spokesperson for the Clinton Foundation, interview with author, October 3, 2011.

AFTERWORD

1   Elizabeth Meyer, "Site Citations," in Carol J. Burns and Andrea Kahn, eds., *Site Matters: Design Concepts, Histories, and Strategies* (New York: Routledge, 2005), 99.

2   In the end only 11 percent of energy use for the Games comes from renewable sources. http://www.huffingtonpost.com/2012/02/19/london-olympic-park-clean-up_n_1283071.html (February 19, 2012), accessed June 10, 2012.

3   After the Games, the management will be taken over the London Legacy Development Corporation, a public body under control of the mayor. If properly funded and managed, this will determine the project's success as a "legacy" plan; however, there is still the question of who benefits (or if enough people benefit) from this type of investment. Olympics are notorious money-losers and yet cities continue to vie for the prestige of hosting the event. Actual costs for London 2012 have been cited as triple to ten times what was estimated.

4   Though practitioners do not control the funding of their work, many are complicit in assuming a particular public by producing images that play into a culture of consumption, laden with lifestyle assumptions and overt "branding." For groups protesting the cost overruns, sponsorship and militarization of the Olympic Games, see Jules Boykoff and Dave Zirin, "Protest Is Coming to the London Olympics," May 21, 2012   http://www.thenation.com/blog/167979/protest-coming-london-olympics#, accessed June 10, 2012.

INDEX

Page numbers in italics represent illustrations.

58; and eighteenth-century aesthetic theory, 142, 223n3; form (topographic formations and dynamism of), 143–47; and Hargreaves Associates' projects that challenge conventional forms of landscape design, 157–58; landscape approaches that invite seasonal water fluctuations (flooding), 16, 99–103, 118, 147–48, 220n25, 221n30; legibility, 143–47, 224n9; Luhmann and, 142–43, 157; Meyer and, 142, 223n3; Olmsted on, 141, 142; perception and communication, 142–43, 157; rhythms and landscapes, 102, 151–56; and seasonal cycles, 16, *20*, 150–51, *181*, *190*; and subjective aesthetic responses to beauty/designed landscapes, 142, 223nn3, 4; topographic forms that invite movement, *152*, 152–53, *194*; and the turn to affect, 225n23. *See also* Louisville Waterfront Park (Louisville, Kentucky); University of Cincinnati Master Plan (Cincinnati, Ohio); William J. Clinton Presidential Center (Little Rock, Arkansas)

Eisenman, Peter: geological approaches, 7–12; and the *imminent* in every site, 8–10; influence, 7–10, 209n20; and mapping, 8–12; use of constructed fragments, 35, *36*; and the void, 10, 209n25; Wexner Center, 35, *36*; on what constitutes a site, 8

Elysian Park, 74–76, *80*. *See also* Los Angeles State Historic Park (LASHP)

emergence, 3, 4, 23; emergent form, 4; emergent material, 4

environmental aesthetics, 3

Environmental Protection Agency (EPA), 218nn10, 14

environmentalism/ environmental movement, 1–3, 93; and changes in construction/ postconstruction practices, 94, 218n11, 219nn12–13; and conservation movement, 93; legislative framework, 93–94, 99, 218nn10–11, 219nn14–15, 221n26. *See also* sustainability/ sustainable landscape design

ethics and landscapes, 106

event spaces, 21–22, *22*, 23, *191*

events, historical (commemoration), 40–44, *41*; and heritage tourism, 42, 215n37; programming geared for diverse groups, 42. *See also* Los Angeles State Historic Park (LASHP); Trail of Tears Passage

Federal Water Pollution Control Act (1948), 218n11

Fens and Riverway (Boston), 219n13

form: clay models, 13, *14–15*, 58, *66*, 107, 184, *188–89*; and construction techniques that avoid naturalistic landscapes, 13, *104*, 104–5; definitions, 144–47; geologic approaches to landscape design, 12–14; and landscape architecture in the 1970s–1980s, 4; and legibility, 143–47; and process-driven approaches, 4–5, 10, 27–28, 44; topographic formations and dynamism of, 143–47, *144–45*, *146*; utopianisms of spatial form, 27–28, 44

fragments. *See* remnants and fragments

Friends of the Los Angeles River (FoLAR), 43, 215n43

function, 217n3; channelization of rivers and different assumptions about, 99–103; functional demands of a landscape (specific and quantifiable tasks), 92, 99, 102–3, 217n3; landscape's performative functions, 19–21

funding for parks, 22, 211n42, 44, 216n47

gabions, 15–16, 100, *123*, *126*

Gas Works Park (Seattle), 2, 35, *36*

geographies (reintroducing time and history into public landscapes), xi, 25–89, 197; and clientele for whom a space is conceived, 42; commemoration of historical events, 40–44; distinction between *consensus* and *collective*, 44; inspiration taken from natural landforms, 29–30, *31*, *32–33*, *34*; letting vacated spaces remain, 27, 44; postindustrial landscapes and urban renewal, 25, 26–28, 212n1; principle of acknowledgment (of a site's past condition), 28–33, 40, 44, 213n13; relics, 35; remnants and fragments, 35–39, 214n26; site legibility and how visitors decode meaning, 30, 143, 213n20; understandings of place, 30–31; and utopianisms of spatial form/utopianisms of process, 27–28, 44; by vertical extension (conceptual connectivity), 29. *See also* Chattanooga Waterfront

geographies *(continued)*
and Renaissance Parks
(Chattanooga, Tennessee);
Crissy Field (San Francisco,
California); Los Angeles State
Historic Park (LASHP)
geological approaches to landscape
design, x, 5–19; avoiding
imitative naturalism, 13,
104–5, 130; clay models, 13,
14–15, 58, *66*, 107, 184,
188–89; cyclical time frames,
16; Eisenman and, 7–12; form,
12–14; Halprin and, 5, 10–11;
Hargreaves Associates' small
plazas, 5–6, *6–7*; mapping,
6, 8–12, *9*, 210n29; material,
15–19; McHarg and, 7–12;
projects that invoke successional
models of growth, 16–19; and
registration, 15; and resistance,
15; sandbox models, *14*; and
the site/site research, 6–8,
10–12, 208n19
Golden Gate National Recreation
Area, 45, *46–51. See also*
Crissy Field (San Francisco,
California)
Government Architect's Design
Directorate (Australia), 107
Guadalupe River Park (San Jose,
California), 92, 99–103,
118–29; Clean Water Act
certification, 103, 222n34;
comparing the diverse
proposals, 99–103, *101*,
220n25; EDAW proposal,
99–100, *101*, 220n25; fluvial
inspired forms acknowledging
the site's past, 29, *34*; funding,
211n44; gabions, 100, *123*,
126; Halprin's first master
plan, 99–100, *101*; Hargreaves
Associates' design (public

landscape/flood control
infrastructure), 99–103, *101*,
118, *120–21*, 220n25, 221n30;
location map, *119*; master plan
showing planting and grading,
120–21; northern areas after
grading, *127*; rhythmic effect
of grasses, landforms, and
shadows, 102, *128–29*; riparian
vegetation, 100, 103, *125*,
126; river channel underneath
freeway, *124*; river flow
capacity, 99–102, 221n27, 30;
sectional differentiation (two
zones), 29, 100–102, 118,
122–23, *126*; terraces and steps,
100, *123*, *126*; USACE flood-
control plan, 99–100, 102,
118, *122–23*, 220n25
Guadalupe River Task Force,
220n25

Halprin, Lawrence, 220n21;
geological approach, 5, 10–11;
Guadalupe River Park first
master plan, 99–100, *101*
Hargreaves, Allen, Sinkosky &
Loomis (HASL), xii
Hargreaves, George, xi; and
acknowledgment of a site's past
condition, 28–29; background
and career, xii; early influences,
3, 4, 10–11, 207n6; early
statement emphasizing process
and open-ended landscape,
4, 5; on the firm's projects as
engagement with program, 147,
224n14; and importance of
mapping, 10–12; on landscape
architectural interventions
in the hydrological cycle, 95;
on narrative nature (allusive
aspect) of the firm's work, 29,
213n19; on postmodernism,

11–12; "Post-Modernism
Looks Beyond Itself" (1983),
11–12, 208n19; and the "rich
history of the ground," 26, 28,
44; on site legibility and how
visitors decode meaning, 30,
143, 213n20; understanding of
place, 30–31; and use of shared
symbols, 28
Harvey, David, 26–28, 207n3,
212n2
heritage tourism, 42, 215n37
history, 2. *See also* geographies
(reintroducing time and history
into public landscapes)

index-maps, 210n29

Jones, Mary Margaret, xii

Krauss, Rosalind, 3, 207n5

landscape, defining, 91; art
critical influences and idea of
landscape in 1970s–80s, 2–4; as
ecological/as technological, 106;
two dominant, contradictory
aspects, 19–21
*Landscape Alchemy: The Work
of Hargreaves Associates*
(Hargreaves et al.), 92, 208n19,
213nn16, 17, 217nn4–5,
223n42, 224n14
landscape architecture
(contemporary): and affect
theory, 225n23; as discipline,
ix–x; engaging the full
range of efficacy, 200–201;
environmental sustainability
and ecofriendly or green design,
ix–x; and public debates over
site use and management,
22–23; socioeconomic
contexts and site conditions,

197; sustainability and energy issues, 197–201; and two contradictory aspects of landscape, 19–21. *See also* geological approaches to landscape design; sustainability/ sustainable landscape design
landscape architecture in the 1970s–1980s, 1–3; art critical influences and idea of landscape, 2–4; ecological turn and a holistic theory of the environment, 1, 3–5, 207n10; and emergence, 3, 4, 23; emphasis on process (formation) over product (form), 4; geological approaches, x, 5–19; history as resource, 2; the postindustrial landscape, 1–2; process-driven design, 3–5, 10; shift in sensibility from modernism to postmodernism, 1, 207n3; structuralism and poststructuralism, 2–3; systems theory, 3–5
landscape urbanism, ix–x, 27, 213n8
LEED (Leadership in Energy and Environmental Design), 217n2
legibility of a site, 30, 143–47, 213n20, 224n9
London Legacy Development Corporation, 225n3
London Olympics (2012), 198–200, *202–3*, 225n3, 226n4; sculpted landforms made from decontaminated on-site soil, 198–200, *202*; sustainability and energy issues, 198–200
Los Angeles River, 74–76, *80, 82,* 215n40
Los Angeles River Revitalization Master Plan (2005–7), 74

Los Angeles State Historic Park (LASHP), 42–44, 74–89; biodiversity strategies, 76, *82–83*; commemoration of historical events, 42–44, 215nn40, 43, 216n46; community participation in development, 43, 213n11; consolidation of high activity areas, 76, *83*; economic analysis based on projections, 216n47; Elysian Park, 74–76, *80*; four large-scale strategies, 76–78, *82–83*; habitat zones, *88*; Hargreaves Associates' proposal (2006–8 schematic design phase), 42–43, 76–89; improving regional connectivity, 76, *81, 82*; interpretive gardens, 43, 76–78, *87, 88*; interpretive pathways and portals, 43, 76–78, *86–87*; interpretive/thematic layers, 43, 76–78, *86–89*, 215n41; media access points, *87*; multi-use lawn, *88–89*; Olmsted-Bartholomew plan (1930), 74; recreational sports fields/ open spaces, 43, 74, 216n45; reestablishing native vegetation, 76, *83*; satellite images, *74–78*; Southern Pacific Rail yard, 43, *84–85*, 215n40; wetlands and stormwater, 76, *82*
Louisville Waterfront Development Corporation (WDC), 158, 211n44
Louisville Waterfront Park (Louisville, Kentucky), 21, 22, 147–48, 152–53, 158–69, *160–61*, 216n46; continuous riverside path, *154–55*, 159; cyclical flooding, 16, 147–48, *148–49*; demarcation between

lawn and flooded zone, 16, 147–48, *148–49, 169*; entry areas and sectional changes, 158–59, *164–65*; events and gathering spaces, 22, *22*; funding and costs, 21, 211n44; grading plan, *163, 164, 166*; Hargreaves Associates' master plan in three phases, 158–59, *162–63*; lawn, *148–49, 165, 167*; linear park and wedge-shaped forms, 152–53, 159, *163, 166–67, 168*; nine-hundred-foot-long fountain, 153, 158–59, *164, 165*; Ohio River, *148–49,* 158–59; overlook terrace, 153, 158, *164*, 167; plantings and trees, 159, *163*; repeating geometries and modified topography, 152–53, *154–55,* 158–59, *166–67*
Luhmann, Nicklas, 142–43, 157

mapping, 6, 8–12, 210n29; Eisenman and, 8–12; geometric, 8–10; geomorphic, 8, *9*; McHarg and, 8, *9*; presumed biases in, 6; transparent overlays, 8, 209n22
material, 15–19; and cyclical time frames, 16, *20*, 147–51; emphasizing striation as opposed to smoothness, 15–19; gabions, concrete, or reinforced edges with geotextiles or groundcover planting, 15–16; projects that invoke successional models of growth, 16–19, *17, 18, 20*; and registration, 15; and resistance, 15. *See also* geological approaches to landscape design
McHarg, Ian, 3, 7–12; *Design with Nature* (1969), 1, 7–8, *9*;

regarding, 94, 219nn14–15; Sydney Olympic Park, 107, *110–11*

Southern Pacific Rail, *84–85*

stormwater: Brightwater's stormwater circuit/collection system, 98, *132–33*, *138–39*; and changes in construction and postconstruction practices, 94, 218n11, 219n12; and constructed wetlands, *70–71*, *73*, *82*, 94, *115*, 219n13; pollutant legislation (nonpoint sources of pollution), 93–94, 218n11

structuralism, 2–3

successional models of growth, 16–19, *17*, *18*, *20*

Superfund (1980), 219n14

sustainability/sustainable landscape design, ix–x, 92, 102–3, 105–6, 197, 221n33; and academic rhetoric concerning landscape urbanism, ix–x; contemporary techniques that attempt to quantify, 92, 102–3, 197, 217n2, 221n33; defining, 92; ecofriendly/green design, ix–x; energy issues, 197–200; how Hargreaves Associates makes use of, 92, 105–6, 217n5; Meyer on, 217n5; notion of fitting/fitness, 106

Sustainable Sites Initiative, 217n2

Sydney Olympic Park (Australia), 92, 95, 107–17; and Bicentennial Park, 107–8; Boundary Creek, 107–8, *111*; design plan, 107–8; Fig Grove fountain, 95, 107, *111*, *116–17*; freshwater wetlands (Northern Water Feature), 95, *96–97*, 107, *111*, *114–15*, 219nn17, 18; historic uses

of the site, 107; location map, *109*; name of, 223n43; Northern Water Feature, 107, *111*, *115*; Olympic Boulevard, *97*, 107–8, *112–13*, *115*, *116*; parklands remediated lands plan, 107, *110–11*; preservation of large trees, 107; soil contamination, 107, *110–11*; study models, 107, *112–13*; water conservation and reuse, 95, *96–97*, 107, *114–15*, 219nn17, 18

systems theory, 3–5

techniques and technologies (to "speed up or slow down" natural processes), xi–xii, 91–139; avoidance of natural-looking/naturalistic landscapes, 13, *104*, 104–5; circulation (interventions in the hydrological cycle), 95–99, *96–97*; constructed wetlands, *70–71*, *73*, *82*, 94, *115*, 219n13; designing intentional mediation between parts of a system, 95–98, 220n21; differentiating "technique" and "technology," 91–92; environmental shift and legislation, 93–94, 99, 218nn10–11, 219nn14–15, 221n26, 222n40; and flow of water, 99–103; and function (functional demands of a landscape), 92, 99, 102–3, 217n3; landscapes as ecological/technological, 106; monotechnics and polytechnics, 93, 105; and program, 92, 147, 217n3, 224n14; resistance (topography as resistive form), 103–5; stabilizing construction/landforms, 104–5, *134*,

136–37; sustainability, 92, 102–3, 105–6, 197, 217n5, 221n33. *See also* Brightwater Wastewater Treatment Facility and Northern Mitigation Area (Snohomish County, Washington); Guadalupe River Park (San Jose, California); Sydney Olympic Park (Australia)

Tennessee River, 58, *60–65*, 68, *70–73*. *See also* Chattanooga Waterfront and Renaissance Parks (Chattanooga, Tennessee)

time. *See* geographies (reintroducing time and history into public landscapes); techniques and technologies (to "speed up or slow down" natural processes)

Trail of Tears Passage, 40–42, *41*, 58–59, *68–69*, 71, 214n33, 215nn35–36. *See also* Chattanooga Waterfront and Renaissance Parks (Chattanooga, Tennessee)

21st Century Waterfront Park. *See* Chattanooga Waterfront and Renaissance Parks (Chattanooga, Tennessee)

University of Cincinnati Master Plan (Cincinnati, Ohio), *170–71*, 170–81; braided path, 151, *180–81*; Campus Green, 151, 172, *178*, *180–81*; challenge of creating a spatially unified campus, 170–72; challenge of negotiating elevation changes, 172, *176*, *178–79*, *180*; conical mounds/landforms, *144–45*, *146*, 151; grading plans, *176*, *178*, *180*; Hargreaves Associates' master plan, 170–72; and history of

ACKNOWLEDGMENTS

I AM GRATEFUL TO THE FOLLOWING ORGANIZATIONS AND INDIVIDUALS WHO HAVE PROVIDED GENEROUS SUPPORT FOR THIS PROJECT: THE GRAHAM FOUNDATION FOR ADVANCED STUDIES IN THE FINE ARTS; FOUNDATION FOR LANDSCAPE STUDIES;

Marilyn Jordan Taylor, dean of the School of Design at the University of Pennsylvania; and James Corner, former chair of the Department of Landscape Architecture at the University of Pennsylvania. At the University of Pennsylvania Press I have had the pleasure of working with Jerry Singerman, Caroline Winschel, Noreen O'Connor-Abel, and Jo Joslyn. In particular, I am grateful to John Dixon Hunt for his early support of this project, his insightful comments along the way, and his patience in seeing it through. I am also indebted to the anonymous readers whose criticisms were tremendously helpful.

I wish to thank colleagues and friends who provided enthusiastic support for the project early on—Pierre Belanger, Alan Berger, Anita Berrizbeitia, David Hays, Gary Hilderbrand, Eric Kramer, and Claudia Taborda. Very special thanks goes to George Hargreaves for providing access to Hargreaves Associates' archive of work but, more importantly, the freedom from "interference" while writing this book. Thank you for your generosity and trust. I would also like to thank the many people at Hargreaves Associates—past and present—who willingly, and quickly, answered my questions and tracked down information for me. There are far too many individuals to name here, but Catherine Miller, Kirt Rieder, and James Smith deserve special mention. My research assistants, Leigh Stewart and Agnes Ladjevardi, were especially helpful.

To the many people who know these landscapes much better than I do: a special thanks to David K. Karem, president of the Louisville Waterfront Development Corporation, for a delightful and illuminating tour of the park and the process of its formation; Gary Pepper, head of maintenance at Louisville Waterfront Park; Jordan Johnson from the Clinton Foundation; and Michael Popiwny from King County. Last, I would like to express my gratitude to two individuals who have provided unwavering support throughout: Caroline Constant, whose critical eye and remarkable editing skills helped sharpen the text—thank you for your generosity of time; and Keith VanDerSys, who patiently read—and reread—drafts, contributed to diagrams in the book, and was a sounding board throughout. Your efforts have helped in immeasurable ways.